EARLY ORGANIZED CRIME IN

DETROIT

VICE, CORRUPTION AND THE RISE OF THE MAFIA

JAMES A. BUCCELLATO

FOREWORD BY SCOTT M. BURNSTEIN

D1496405

THE
History
PRESS

Published by The History Press
Charleston, SC
www.historypress.net

First published 2015

Manufactured in the United States

ISBN 978.1.46711.754.8

Library of Congress Control Number: 2015950780

CONTENTS

FOREWORD

Early Organized Crime in Detroit is an important book by an important author. The early days of the Detroit underworld were groundbreaking and sent ripple effects throughout the entire United States of America. Some of them are still felt today. Dr. James Buccellato is a seminal researcher in this field and the main authority on the subject in Michigan. The fresh insights he provides in this project and the extensive detail he goes into to flesh out the fascinating roots of mob activity in the Great Lakes region only builds on the already-rich tapestry that surrounds it and cements his first book effort as a smashing success and key teaching tool for the future.

James and I are kindred spirits, and I'm proud to call him a friend and colleague. We met at one of my book signings several years ago and immediately hit it off. I knew I had found an instant "partner in crime." Our collaborations are some of the highlights of my career. I consider the chapter we co-wrote in my third book (*Detroit True Crime Chronicles*) delving into international drug smuggling in Detroit in the 1950s and 1960s a crowning achievement in my personal publishing endeavors.

The Motor City in the first part of the twentieth century was as influential nationwide in criminality as it was for birthing the automotive industry. During Prohibition, Detroit became the epicenter of bootlegging activity in America due to the area's proximity to Canada. Immediately after Prohibition, the Detroit underworld transformed itself into ground zero for the North American narcotics industry and mob infiltration of organized labor. This led to watershed gangland innovation in and throughout

FOREWORD

Southeast Michigan, lending to its well-earned reputation as unique mafia and street gang terrain. So unique, in fact, specifically in terms of bloodlines, that many of the same names of the men who ran the mob in Detroit in the 1920s and 1930s were or are still in charge of the rackets well into the new millennium. The names Tocco, Corrado, Palazzolo, Bommarito, D'Anna, Meli and Mirabile remain prominent in Detroit mafia circles in 2015, just as they were almost one hundred years ago.

Local crime lords reached tremendous heights of power, and the allegiances and rivalries they forged were complex. With his exceptional authorship and research, Buccellato places them in proper context while shedding new light on them and providing a stellar, pinpoint analysis of the whys, whos, whats and wheres. If you are someone who appreciates the study of history, politics, the mob, the labor movement or sociology, this is a must-read.

SCOTT M. BURNSTEIN
Author, historian, investigative journalist
August 2015

ACKNOWLEDGEMENTS

There is not enough room in these pages to express my gratitude to everyone who made this book possible. I will do my best, however, to say thank you to the following people: I have to thank my loving, creative and patient wife, Kristen. There would be no book without her kindness, insight and belief in me. I want to thank the Boschian, Karth, Malec, Malecki and Paga families for their generosity and enthusiastic support. I am especially grateful to Karen for conducting research at the Brooklyn Public Library.

Special appreciation goes to Scott M. Burnstein. His pioneering research inspired me to take on crime as a research agenda. He is a generous friend and "co-conspirator." David Critchley is another researcher who deserves special thanks. Critchley's research on the Detroit mafia motivated me to dig deeper into my ancestry. David helped me get started with my research, and I am extremely grateful. Other researchers who were more than kind along the way include Justin Vitiello, Lennert Van 't Riet, Richard Warner and Angelo Santino. I also thank Mike Tona, Mike Rizzo, Al Bradley, Westin Pulizzi, Bill Feather and "Barbarian."

I am grateful to Jerry Herron, Kevin Rashid, Stuart May and the Irvin D. Reid Honors College at Wayne State University for their generous support of this project. I also thank my Honors partners in crime: Kevin Ball, Justin Rex, Aaron Martin, Elizabeth Hudson, Beth Fowler and Kevin Deegan-Krause. A number of other Wayne State University colleagues deserve recognition. I can never thank Nora Jarbou and Cinzia Acciani enough for their research assistance and help with translations.

ACKNOWLEDGEMENTS

Even more importantly, they are my friends. Thanks to Anna Yaldo for mapping out Detroit crime scenes.

The following archivists and librarians deserve exceptional praise for assisting my work: Judith Arnold and Cynthia Krolikowski and the Wayne State University libraries, Elizabeth Clemens and the Walter P. Reuther Library, Jill Arnold and the entire staff at the State Archives of Michigan, Joann Mannino and the Detroit Public Library, Umberto Santino and the Centro Siciliano di Documentazione in Palermo, Sicily.

I am privileged to be a member of the Buccellato family and have to thank my North American and Sicilian relatives. Fred, Dawn, Fiora, Rose, Rosa, Peter, Marie, Vita Marie, Flora, Laura, Jim, Vita, Chase and my father deserve special acknowledgement for sharing the family history with me. I hope you enjoy the book. I also thank the Bonanno/Labruzzo family (Gary Abromovitz, Bambi, Rosalie and Anthony) for their hospitality when I was in Tuscon.

Finally, I thank Krista Slavicek and The History Press for their guidance and confidence in this book.

CHAPTER I

"THERE IS NO MAFIA IN DETROIT"

Giuseppe Noto's head was nearly severed when investigators found his body on November 19, 1901. The murder occurred in Springfield, Illinois, but detectives on the case believed the main suspect, Filippo Tocco, was hiding in Detroit. Tocco initially fled to St. Louis, where he had relatives, but after a few days, he left for Detroit, seeking the protective shelter of friends in the area. Eleven days after the murder, Detroit detective Ferdinand Palma heard rumors that Tocco was holed up at a house on Macomb Street. As one of Detroit's most prominent Italian residents, Palma knew most of his fellow immigrants living in the area known as Little Sicily (or the Italian colony). As a result, an unfamiliar face like Tocco's would stand out in the close-knit community.

After searching a handful of homes, Palma discovered an individual he didn't recognize. Moreover, the person acted nervous as Palma asked about his identity and purpose in Detroit. The detective brought the stranger in for questioning. The suspect gave an assumed name but soon admitted to Palma that he was the man police were seeking. Tocco admitted his identity but vehemently denied the murder charges. He claimed he had acted in self-defense. Even more provocative, however, Filippo Tocco claimed that he and Giuseppe Noto were members of an Italian secret society known as the mafia.

Detroit skyline as seen from Windsor, Canada, circa 1910. *Library of Congress.*

Two Murders

Such a startling revelation stimulated conversations among members of the Italian community, journalists covering the case and police investigators. Observers wondered if they were witnessing another "mafia outbreak" like the one that had taken place in New Orleans. The "outbreak" referred to a series of tragic events that occurred in 1890. When New Orleans police chief David Hennessy was murdered, the police department and citizens alike suspected that a secret society of Italian criminals was responsible. One year later, nine Italian men were tried for the murder of Chief Hennessy. The wider community was outraged when the jury acquitted the men on all charges. Angry residents stormed the parish prison looking to exact revenge. Overall, nine Italians were shot to death execution style, while two others were dragged outside and lynched.

Back in Detroit, Palma wanted to assure everyone that there was no such phenomenon occurring in his city. According to the detective, the mafia was a four-hundred-year-old self-protection society operating in Sicily. He explained the group emerged as a response to injustices carried out by occupying governments. Throughout Sicily's history, various armies and royal states traded places conquering and ruling the island. So for Palma, the mafia existed in some type of gray area between vigilante group and national liberation militia. Regardless, he told reporters that the only Sicilian society in Detroit was the "sick and death benefit organization." He added, "You can say for me that there is no Mafia in Detroit."

Still, as details regarding the Noto murder came forth, the term "mafia" lingered in the public consciousness. Tocco even backed away from his earlier self-proclaimed affiliation and accused Giuseppe Noto of being the only Mafioso in question. He said the society tried to recruit him back in Sicily, but he refused to join. Noto, on the other hand, was a killer operating in Texas and New Orleans, at least according to Tocco. Investigators realized the men had worked together at the Alton Railroad Corporation in Illinois. The murder suspect reported that during their last job, the employer had only enough cash to pay one of the two men. According to his story, the employer paid Tocco rather than Noto and a fight ensued. Tocco claimed Noto pulled a knife and demanded he hand over the money. Tocco claimed he wrestled the blade away and stabbed Noto in self-defense. Investigators were not buying the story. In fact, they believed their suspect was the true mafia killer and Noto an extortion target and murder victim. On May 31, 1902, Tocco was found guilty and sentenced to fifteen years.

Palma's message regarding the mafia's nonexistence was successful, and no moral panic developed in Detroit. Nevertheless, two years later, another murder in Little Sicily produced sensationalistic headlines and suggested things were more complicated than Palma acknowledged.

Matteo Palazzolo was shot to death on December 27, 1904. It was seven o'clock in the evening when the thirty-two-year-old Palazzolo entered John White's home on Hastings Street. Within minutes, Palazzolo was dying from a bullet wound in his neck.

Detective Palma arrived on the scene and arrested everyone in the house, including Giuseppe Caladrino, Vito Badalucco, Luigi Liberatore, John White and Rosina Romail. The home belonged to White and Romail, who lived as common-law man and wife. Romail was known in the neighborhood as a type of healer. Her mixes of holistic herbs and medicines were popular in the community.

On the night in question, Matteo Palazzolo, along with Caladrino and Badalucco, entered the White residence and accused Romail of selling sham products. When Romail protested and told the men to leave, Palazzolo and his crew threw the woman on the bed. Hearing the ruckus, John White and his brother Luigi Liberatore rushed in and claimed Palazzolo drew his pistol. He fired once, hitting Liberatore in the neck. Romail ran outside screaming for help as more gunfire was exchanged inside the home. According to police reports, seven shots were fired altogether. One individual was dead, and another was critically wounded.

Trying to put the pieces together, Palma initially suspected the gunfight was the result of interethnic conflict. It turned out that White and his brother were from Naples, while Palazzolo, Caladrino and Badalucco were Sicilian. Complicating things further, Rosina Romail was from Calabria. Palma was looking at individuals from three distinct regions of Italy, each with its own entrenched traditions of banditry, secret societies and vendetta. Moreover, there was no love lost between Italians from the respective regions. After interviewing Romail, Palma realized the incident had less to do with regional rivalries and more to do with an organization he maintained did not exist in Detroit.

Romail's allegations were shocking. According to Romail, she had escaped a human trafficking ring and was on the run from the "dreaded mafia." In fact, "Rosina Romail" was an alias she used to conceal her real identity. Her plight had started back in Calabria, Italy, where she was forced into marriage at fourteen years old. Not long after the marriage, Romail's husband left for Austria seeking employment but never returned. Left destitute, Rosina thought she met a guardian angel when an Italian American traveling in Calabria told her about economic opportunities across the Atlantic. He told her his brother in Brooklyn was looking for a bride. Rosina Romail would have access to economic prosperity and citizenship in New York; all she had to do was marry the stranger's brother.

Rosina traveled with the man to Brooklyn, yet she soon realized the arrangement was a scam. There was no brother, no marriage and no prosperity. The man she linked up with was a human trafficker. Once in New York, he turned Romail into an indentured servant. He made it clear that he would "cut her head off" if she tried to escape. Adding to her dread, she suspected the man was a member of the mafia.

The details are unclear, but at some point, Romail managed to escape from the Brooklyn housing resort where she was being held. While on the run, she met John White and explained her predicament. The two fell in love, and White agreed the couple should escape to Canada. They fled to Montreal, but the human traffickers found her there and threatened to kill her if she didn't buy her freedom. Somehow the couple dodged

A rare image of Detroit's Little Sicily neighborhood during the early 1900s. *Walter P. Reuther Library.*

their tormentors and fled again. They headed southwest to Toronto and eventually made it to Detroit.

Detective Palma found the woman's harrowing tale convincing. As a result, the Detroit Police Department dropped all charges against John White and his brother. Romail, White and Liberatore left the city immediately.

The case produced front-page news in Detroit but also raised a troubling issue. Investigators believed the attack on Romail was linked to an extortion plot rather than a conflict over shoddy healing products. Reporters wondered if mafia operatives were active in Detroit after all. Consequently, journalists, police investigators and the local clergy continued to debate and discuss what exactly this shadowy brotherhood represented and how it functioned. To better comprehend the phenomenon, Detroiters had to understand the city's Italian colony.

EARLY ORGANIZED CRIME IN DETROIT

THE ITALIAN COLONY

During the summer of 1895, the *Detroit Free Press* published a detailed account of the city's emerging Italian community. The article mapped out the parameters of the immigrant colony. Extending a few blocks north of the Detroit River to Larned Street and east of Woodward Avenue, one would find a swath of Italian neighborhoods lined up between Brush and Beaubien Street. Eventually, the colony would expand north and produce neighborhoods between Gratiot and Mack Avenues. In a few years, Italian residential areas expanded east to Chene Street as well.

Ten years earlier, the newspaper had counted over one thousand Italian immigrants in the area. By 1895, the population had doubled to over two thousand. The *Free Press* pointed out the Italian section was relatively small compared to other ethnic enclaves in the city. German, Irish and Polish communities were much larger during this period. Unlike other big cities, ethnic sections in Detroit were never completely homogeneous. Even in the so-called Italian colony, Jews, Poles, Germans and black Americans lived nearby.

Still, Italians were concentrated enough to give the colony some distinct ethnic characteristics. Reporters described walking up and down Rivard Street watching families eat the common lunch of *pomodori* and *mortadella*. There was an active commercial center, and one could hear gentlemen playing the hand organ in the background as street peddlers interacted with their customers. The newspaper described the neighborhoods as clean and its residents as stoic. "It is noticeable that these Italians do not complain of hard times," wrote the *Free Press*.

Members of the community took their Catholic faith seriously. Sicilian Detroiters would not get their own Catholic church until Holy Family Church opened in 1910. In the meantime, parishioners attended services at Peter and Paul's Jesuit Church near the riverfront. The colony's most important social activities—such as marriage, baptism and confirmation—centered on religion. Churches offered English lessons and cooking classes as well. Meanwhile, some Italians attended Protestant services. The Jefferson Avenue Presbyterian Church hosted night school classes for Italian men in coordination with the Young Men's Christian Association. In additional to spiritual lessons, the night classes offered job training and placement services.

Other organizations important to the community included mutual aid societies like the *Societa' di Unione e Fratellanza Italiana*, founded in 1873. The Garibaldi Society of Mutual Benefit was another organization that helped members of the community by treating the sick and reducing healthcare

Street Tenement District in Palermo, circa 1910. Most of the Sicilians immigrating to Detroit were from Palermo and surrounding towns. *Library of Congress.*

costs. In 1873, Italian laborers formed their own employees' union, known as the Union Brotherhood.

Italians actually had a presence in Detroit going back to the arrival of Atonine de la Mothe Cadillac in 1704. Alphonse De Tonty from Gaeta, Italy, was one of Cadillac's top lieutenants. The first major wave of Italian immigration, however, did not occur until the 1850s. Most of these immigrants originated in the city of Genoa, a coastal town in Northern Italy. Soon, a number of families from the northern region of Lombardy settled in Detroit. Sicilians represented the next major wave of Italian immigration in the 1880s. Like other European immigrants, they settled in Detroit seeking better economic opportunities.

Prior to the establishment of the automotive industry, Detroit had already emerged as a manufacturing hub. By 1900, for example, Detroit featured nine drug manufacturers and over twenty metal-related factories, including brass, cooper, iron and steel works. The city was also home to dozens of furniture, food, clothing, tobacco and silverware factories. The co-emergence of industrialization and immigration led to the creation of numerous other jobs in the service and infrastructure sectors.

Such economic growth positioned Detroit as an ideal destination for Europeans seeking better lives. Accordingly, by 1900, approximately one-third of Detroit's 286,000 residents were immigrants. Newly arriving Sicilians were actually underrepresented in the manufacturing sector. Sicilian immigrants often found themselves employed as laborers in the construction trades. Newspaper accounts mention that a prominent number of Italians worked digging sewers and ditches to accommodate the rapid growth of the city. Others worked as street peddlers, while Italians with access to more capital opened restaurants and grocery stores. Some worked as artisans, and the community featured a handful of physicians, pharmacists, police officers and college professors.

At the turn of the century, the Italian population increased yet again, expanding to five thousand residents. Though Italians composed less than 2 percent of the city's population, it was clear they represented an industrious and creative community that enhanced the overall quality of Detroit.

SECRET SOCIETIES

Even as newspaper accounts highlighted the appealing characteristics of the Italian colony, observers also noted some peculiar features. Editorial writers were concerned about perceived "traces of folk-lore, customs, folk-laws, and superstitions from fiery Sicily." The *Detroit Free Press* was quite judgmental, writing, "Perhaps the most absurd of these follies is the Sicilian belief in the 'evil eye.'" According to Sicilian folk tradition, individuals used the sign of the *malocchio* to either ward off evil energies or curse an enemy, depending on the circumstances. For editorial writers, industrial Detroit represented the high point of modernity; subsequently, there was no room in the city for "primitive" superstitions from the Old World.

Reporters also expressed concern about the Italian community importing the mafia and the "vendetta" from Sicily. Newspapers were already talking about the mafia, but an editorial in 1907 introduced two new concepts: the Camorra and the Black Hand. At this point, it wasn't clear how the mafia, Camorra and Black Hand differed from one another, but it was understood that each was a type of criminal organization. The idea of vendetta or blood feud was certainly not unique to Sicilian culture. The Albanians, Greeks, Irish, Scots and Turks, among others, featured bloody rivalries throughout their respective cultural histories. Even America had the Hatfields and the McCoys. So blood feuds and bandits were universal cultural characteristics. Nevertheless, the mafia was something different. This was a uniquely Sicilian construct, and observers tried to comprehend how this entity functioned.

In 1904, the *Detroit Free Press* published an article on the subject by H. Riversdale Coghlan. The piece represented one of the earliest and best descriptions of the mafia written in English. Coghlan was somewhat of a mystery man. He studied theology in England and was involved in some type of fieldwork in Italy, but the context is unclear. Either way, he offered a remarkably accurate account of the mafia, even by today's scholarship. His article shed light on crucial elements of the Sicilian fraternity.

First, Coghlan identified similarities between Freemasonry and the mafia. He maintained we shouldn't view the organization as a political group "nor as a purely criminal one." Instead, like the Freemasons, the mafia was an opportunity for men of status to network with one another. Such networking presented opportunities for members to enhance their economic holdings and secure political favors. Yet this was not an informal social organization. Also like Freemasonry, the mafia maintained strict membership requirements and incorporated elaborate rituals into its initiation ceremonies. Coghlan wrote, "Before a man can join the mafia he has to go through a series of strict probationary trials." If the prospective member was deemed worthy, he participated in a specific induction ceremony. Here Coghlan described the event: "After smearing an image of his favorite saint with blood drawn from his body, [he] sets the image on fire and takes the following oath: I swear on my honor to be faithful to the brotherhood. As this saint and the drops of my blood are destroyed, so I will shed all my blood for the fraternity."

Importantly, Coghlan recognized that membership in the organization transcended political affiliations and professional distinctions. Fidelity to the brotherhood trumped all other social concerns. He also cautioned readers to avoid conflating Mafiosi with ordinary bandits. Members may have engaged in theft and extortion, but the ends were different for the Mafioso.

He employed such methods to control the distribution of resources. By controlling access to land, grain, water, livestock and produce, the Mafioso positioned himself as the most important man in town.

Again, it is unclear how Coghlan acquired such valuable insight, but it seems plausible he was familiar with the investigations of Ermanno Sangiorgi. The 1890s were a tumultuous time for Italy. The nation experienced economic instability combined with rampant public corruption. Reform politicians in Rome suspected the Sicilian mafia was responsible for engineering the crisis. In 1898, Italian prime minister Luigi Pelloux named Ermanno Sangiorgi Palermo's new chief of police. Sangiorgi was charged with gathering as much intelligence as possible on Sicily's criminal underworld. The new police chief accumulated a significant amount of evidence and produced what is known as the Sangiorgi Report.

His research matched Coghlan's analysis well. Sangiorgi uncovered evidence about secret ceremonies and blood rituals. The report explained how Mafiosi used intimidation and murder to maintain monopolies on resource distribution. Palermo's police chief also illustrated for the first time how the mafia organized itself. The mafia actually existed as a network of independent cells (or families) linked to specific territories. Each family adhered to a specific hierarchical model. The top of the administration consisted of a boss (*capo*), an underboss (*sotocapo*) and an advisor (*consigliere*). Operating below the ruling council were captains (*capodecina*). Each captain was responsible for a group of ten soldiers (*soldati*).

Prime Minister Pelloux also wanted Sangiorgi to gather information on specific Mafiosi. Pelloux suspected that a certain member of Parliament was a member. Reformers believed this politician wasn't just a rank-and-file member either. They argued he was Palermo's most powerful Mafioso. His name was Raffaele Palizzolo. By the summer of 1908, don Raffaele was on his way to Detroit.

CHAPTER 2

BANDITS AND DONS

On June 21, 1908, members of Detroit's leading Sicilian civic organizations convened for a meeting and passed the following resolution: "Palizzolo is not welcome in Detroit." Members from the following civic groups sent representatives to the meeting: the Italian Workers' Union, Dante Alighieri Society, *La Trinacria*, *Duca Abruzzi* and *Casa Savoia*. Leaders and general members from the organizations met at the Italian Union Workers' Hall on Russell Street. The gathering was called by local community power broker Francesco Paolo D'Anna. He wanted the Sicilian colony to sanction a visit by the prominent Italian politician Commendatore Raffaele Palizzolo.

According to D'Anna and his supporters, this was an excellent opportunity to showcase the growing Italian colony to a foreign dignitary. Palizzolo was the son of a baroness and powerful member of the Italian Parliament. D'Anna reasoned that bringing such a distinguished public figure to Detroit would generate favorable publicity for the community. Organizers of the meeting expected unanimous support but badly miscalculated. Instead, the meeting nearly ended in bedlam. Attendees started shouting and pushing and shoving one another. D'Anna's supporters actually feared for his life and escorted him out of the building. Overall, the organizations passed a resolution condemning Palizzolo.

So what was the hullabaloo about? Proponents of Palizzolo's visit overlooked an important fact: large numbers of Sicilians in both Italy and Detroit considered don Raffaele a dangerous Mafioso.

DON RAFFAELE VISITS DETROIT

Back in Sicily, Palizzolo was a man of great wealth and status. Sicilians referred to such men as *uomini di rispetto*—men of respect. According to historian John Dickie, "Don Raffaele Palizzolo would receive his clients in the morning in his Palermo home in the Palazzo Villarosa." Today, the magnificent palace is open to the public and hosts banquets, weddings and conferences. In don Raffaele's time, however, clients and constituents traveled to the palace seeking personal favors and public support from the don. He was well placed to grant such patronage and goodwill. Born into an aristocratic family, Palizzolo was close to powerful public figures like Prime Minister Francesco Crispi. Through his bloodline and political connections, don Raffaele accumulated large amounts of real estate. He made a fortune leasing the land to citrus farmers. Palizzolo was involved in philanthropy and held a number of public positions, including director of the merchant navy's health insurance fund and trustee of the Sicilian National Bank.

A beloved figure to some, others accused Palizzolo of using nefarious alliances to sustain and expand his power. Critics alleged the don was connected to local mafia families. Others went further and accused Palizzolo of being a high-ranking member of the Sicilian criminal brotherhood. His biggest critic was Marquis Emanuele Notarbartolo. During his tenure as mayor of Palermo, Notarbartolo clashed with don Raffaele on numerous occasions. The mayor accused Palizzolo of embezzling funds from his various charitable endeavors. Notarbartolo even forced his rival to publicly return the ill-gotten loot. Furthermore, he alleged Palizzolo regularly used his political privileges to protect mafia-linked bandits.

On February 1, 1893, Notarbartolo was taking a train from Sciara to Palermo. The first-class compartment was empty, and the former mayor was without a bodyguard. Believing bandits would not attack someone on a train in a metropolitan area, he placed his rifle on the rack above the seats. At some point between the Termini and Trabia stops, two men attacked Notarbartolo and stabbed him to death.

Throughout the investigation, it seemed that powerful interests were intervening and obstructing the pursuit of justice. Nevertheless, six years after the crime, the murder trial of Emanuele Notarbartolo was underway. Provocatively, during his testimonial, Notarbartolo's son issued the following charge: "I believe that the murder was a vendetta and that the only man who hated my father is Commendatore Raffaele Palizzolo."

R. PALIZZOLO, LEADER OF THE MAFIA.

Don Raffaele Palizzolo. Born into aristocracy, Palizzolo was also a powerful Mafioso. *Author's collection.*

Such a shocking pubic accusation created a media sensation. Notarbartolo's son was a respected naval officer and not prone to flippancy. Consequently, Italy's political elite could not dismiss the allegations outright. Bowing to public pressure, Prime Minister Pelloux stripped Palizzolo of his seat in Parliament. Don Raffaele was no longer protected by Parliamentary immunity and was now in the cross hairs of investigators. The murder trial continued in Milan, and Palizzolo was tried as a co-conspirator. Finally, in 1902, the court reached a verdict: Palizzolo was found guilty of ordering the murder of Emanuele Notarbartolo. The verdict produced more media sensationalism, while anti-mafia reformers viewed this is a significant blow against organized crime.

Six months later, however, don Raffaele proved too cagey for Italy's anti-crime crusaders. The Court of Cassation in Rome overturned the verdict on a technicality. Palizzolo was re-tried in 1903 and this time acquitted on all charges. Don Raffaele returned to Palermo triumphantly.

A few years later, the don decided to spend his semi-retirement touring the United States. Before making his way to Detroit, the commendatore visited New York City. Palizzolo's visit to the Big Apple was not contentious like his Detroit stop, yet New Yorkers were aware of the don's dubious reputation. The *New York Times* had covered the Notabartolo murder trial years earlier. Once again, the newspaper examined Palizzolo, only this time the don was in America. The *Times* described him as a "stout gentleman of 63 years old, with grey hair and mustache." Reporters noted he was soft spoken with "penetrating" eyes.

Ironically, while in the city, the don traveled with famous New York police detective Joe Petrosino. The detective acted as Palizzolo's bodyguard during his stay. Petrosino was undoubtedly the most well-known anti-mafia crusader in law enforcement at the time. In 1903, he famously arrested one of America's original mafia bosses, don Vito Cascio Ferro. Petrosino, however, was unapologetic about his new travel acquaintance. The detective viewed the bodyguard assignment as a privilege and described Palizzolo as "a man of blood, of action, a gentleman, and a scholar."

Though Palizzolo was keeping good company, reporters asked don Raffaele about his alleged criminal associations. He denied belonging to any criminal secret society but did provide an alternative description of the mafia. Whereas writers like Coghlan and investigators like Sangiorgi emphasized the mafia's predatory wealth accumulation and secret blood rituals, Palizzolo offered a romantic and nationalistic interpretation. Don Raffaele claimed the secret society traced its origins to 1282 and the War of the Sicilian Vespers. The event referred to an anti-colonial rebellion by Sicilians against King Charles I and his French occupiers. According to one legend, a French solider attempted to sexually assault a Sicilian woman on her wedding day. The groom responded by bludgeoning the solider with his knife. During the ruckus, the Sicilian shouted out, "*Morte ai Francesi, Italia anela!*" (Death to the French, Italy cries out). Stringing together the first letter of each word in Italian spells out "mafia." The singular incident signified a larger conflict, namely the French exploitation of the Sicilian people. Furthermore, the husband's act of defiance ignited a wider political resistance against colonial rule.

Some of Detroit's most important Mafiosi were from Castellammare Del Golfo, Cinisi and Terrasini. *Author's collection.*

Buying into such folklore, Palizzolo claimed the mafia traced its origins to collective acts of mutual aid during times of oppression. He asked reporters, "Suppose you lived in a county where the disposition of life and property of the individual was in the hands of a few who used their power for personal profit and for the gratification of personal ambition, would you not attempt to remedy this wrong—by force if necessary?" According to such logic, the mafia was primarily concerned with justice, and Palizzolo even compared Sicilian vigilantes to the American Revolutionaries.

The don enjoyed his visit to New York and encouraged Italian immigrants to learn English, embrace America and avoid associating with criminal elements. Palizzolo hoped to sell this positive message to Detroiters, yet clearly a strong vocal opposition had emerged inside the Sicilian colony. Even though rank-and-file members of Detroit's Italian organizations passed a resolution denouncing Palizzolo, a faction of civic leaders held their ground and invited the divisive figure. Don Raffaele's supporters in Detroit formed their own committee featuring local businessman Francesco D'Anna, Tony Orlando (a close associate of Detective Ferdinand Palma) and Joseph Marino (the president of *Casa Savoia*).

Committee members welcomed their guest of honor on July 17, 1908. D'Anna and his delegation met Palizzolo at the train station and shuttled him to C.G. Andruzzi's Italian restaurant on Six Mile Road. After dinner, the party gave don Raffaele a tour of Detroit. Once downtown, Commendatore Palizzolo reached his final destination of the evening: the Hotel Pontchartrain. There he stayed in Parlor E, one of the hotel's most plush rooms. According to reporters, Don Raffaele was "handsomely entertained" by the party of local Italian leaders.

The press continued to acknowledge the Italian community's mixed reactions to the controversial visitor. Even restaurateur C.G. Adruzzi expressed ambivalence regarding Palizzolo. Adruzzi, who was also a county clerk, was honored to host such a high-profile guest in his restaurant. He nevertheless acknowledged, "His visit is certainly unwelcome by the majority of Italians here." Newspapers described a split between local Italian elites and populist opposition. According to the *Free Press*, "a good two-thirds of the Italian colony" was keenly opposed to don Raffaele's visit. Labor activists and Italian intellectuals provided the most vocal criticism. The opposition formed its own committee featuring civic leader and *Risorgimento* president Giuseppe Sansone, Italian Workers' Union president Alfred Franchi and socialist activist Antonio Buscemi. Referring to Palizzolo, Franchi told reporters: "He is the head of the mafia and the Black Hand." He added, "We Italians in America love our country and we do not want the Americans to think that we countenance those movements by inviting such a man as Palizzolo to visit and by paying him honor as a great man. We resent it and we propose to let the public know that we resent it."

Nevertheless, don Raffaele and his supporters continued on as planned. His welcoming committee hosted a banquet in his honor at the Hotel Pontchartrain. The soirée featured a handful of prominent non-Italian Detroiters, including Mayor William Thompson, Judge William F. Connolly, county treasurer Captain George Waldo and high-profile attorney James Murtha. With Ferdinand Palma acting as his interpreter, Palizzolo told the party he appreciated the beauty and hospitality of Detroit. In fact, he claimed the city inspired him to write a book about America. As for his critics, he dismissed them as "socialists" and "politically motivated."

For his final day in Detroit, Palizzolo's committee scheduled a speaking engagement for their guest at the Light Infantry Armory located at the corner of Larned and Brush Street. Newspapers reported that the seven hundred audience members underwent "rigid security" to attend the event. Reporters asked Joseph Marino if he feared "anarchists" would target Palizzolo and

The famous Hotel Pontchartrain located in downtown Detroit. Don Raffaele Palizzolo held court here during his visit. *Library of Congress.*

disrupt the event. Marino rejected the idea that Sicilians engaged in radical politics and insisted the opposition was based on petty jealousies. Marino nevertheless took strict safety measures and confronted three audience members before the speech. Marino identified Alfred Franchi's wife in the audience, along with two members of the Italian Workers' Union.

Palizzolo delivered his speech as scheduled and, according to newspaper coverage, was well received. Don Raffaele singled out Giuseppe Sansone and the IWU for stirring up opposition to his visit. Palizzolo claimed their criticisms were unfounded and vehemently denied any connections to organized crime or the Black Hand. He did offer some interesting coded language, however. After denying he was a Mafioso, don Raffaele told his audience, "But even were I guilty, the man who would circulate such charges against me in a foreign land is not a good Sicilian and should be disowned by his countrymen." Essentially, the don was reminding his audience members about *omerta*—the Sicilian code of silence. Whether Palizzolo was a criminal or not, the point was that Sicilians should not discuss such matters with outsiders.

Early Organized Crime in Detroit

The commendatore left Detroit, and political tensions deescalated. Interestingly though, the term "Black Hand" seemed to haunt don Raffaele's visit as much as the word "mafia." Palizzolo himself urged Italians in America to resist the Black Hand. After the clamor regarding his visit subsided, the notion of a mafia in Detroit started to lose its cachet with reporters and investigators. Instead, the city focused on the dreaded *La Mano Nera*.

Reign of Terror

Police detectives confronted Gaspare Reani at midnight in front of St. Mary's Church on Monroe Avenue. Reani resisted arrest and pulled out an eight-inch dagger. After slashing one of the officers, he reached for his revolver and stuck the pistol in the belly of the other detective. Fortunately for the detective, Reani dropped his gun before firing a shot. The officers finally wrestled the weapons away from the suspect and brought him downtown for questioning.

The confrontation developed out of a sting operation. Earlier in the day, an Italian Detroiter named Joseph Rizzo entered police headquarters and declared he was the victim of a Black Hand extortion plot. Rizzo had received a letter claiming that if he didn't pay $2,000, he would pay with his life. The letter instructed the victim to appear at St. Mary's Church at 1:00 a.m. to drop off the payment. Rizzo claimed he'd been receiving threatening letters for some time and hoped the authorities would intervene. A police surveillance team staked out the drop location, and Reani appeared around midnight.

Not long after Reani was apprehended, Ferdinand Palma arrived at police headquarters to interrogate the suspect. Palma knew of Reani but could not say if the suspect had a criminal background. He knew the extortionist had arrived in Detroit in 1905 and worked a variety of labor jobs, including a brief stint at the Hotel Pontchartrain. Other than that, Reani was a mystery. Palma wanted to make clear, however, that the so-called Black Hand was not a national criminal conspiracy. He added, "There is no such thing as the 'Black Hand' as an organization." Instead, Palma argued, the city was dealing with a few individual cutthroats and crooks looking to exploit their fellow Italian immigrants.

Unfortunately for those in the Italian colony, examples like the attempted extortion of Joseph Rizzo were becoming common. By 1908, threatening letters were circulating throughout the community, usually followed by acts of arson and bombings. Each note was signed *Mano Nera* (Black Hand) and featured a variety of designs. Letters usually centered on menacing images—daggers, swords, skulls and crosses being the most common.

Newspapers reported how Black Handers firebombed Pietro Mercurio's home after he refused to pay the extortion fee. The arsonists then went after his brother Antonio Mercurio and set fire to his grocery store. Black Handers tried to extort civic leader Giuseppe Sansone and burned down his barn when he refused to pay. No longer feeling safe in Detroit, Joseph Rizzo and the Mercurio brothers fled back to Sicily.

Investigators estimated that victims paid out between $10,000 and $20,000 in extortion fees to the Black Hand. One newspaper account described a saloonkeeper who started packing two revolvers "at all times" once he started receiving letters. "His wife carried a revolver in her waist and a stiletto in her stocking," added the reporter. Like Rizzo and the Mercurio brothers, the saloonkeeper eventually shut down his business and moved back to Italy.

During an exposé on the Black Hand, the *Detroit Free Press* labeled Little Sicily the "region of terror." Yet Detroit wasn't the only city experiencing the extortion outbreak. Cities with large Italian populations like Chicago and New York were dealing with similar problems. Even smaller towns in Ohio and Pennsylvania reported Black Hand incidents. In each city, the gang's formula was similar: send a threatening letter with menacing images, demanding payment. The extortionist might even write several letters before engaging in any violent acts. Usually the Black Hand employed arson and bombings as tactics rather than beatings or shootings. In terms of targeting their victims, the bandits were equal opportunists. Sometimes they knew the victim and had prior knowledge of the target's personal wealth. In other cases, the target was random and the crook asked for unrealistic sums of money considering the victim's actual financial status.

Father Giovanni Boschi, arguably the most influential spiritual leader in the community, claimed to be "mystified" by the rash of extortion threats. Boschi arrived in Detroit in 1907 and had already established himself as an important member of the Italian colony. He taught at Detroit College and founded a parish for Sicilians at Peter and Paul's Jesuit Church. Boschi already knew of fifty families extorted by the Black Hand. He compared these Italian criminals to the old American outlaws. "They are probably men who have worn chains in penitentiaries across the seas, men determined not to work," added Boschi. He stated it was imperative that Sicilian residents come forward and provide information to the proper authorities.

In addition to calling on Italian Detroiters to cooperate with law enforcement, community leaders like Palma and Boschi agreed *La Mano Nera* was not part of some national criminal network. Boschi stated that the Black Hand as "an extended organization…does not exist, either here or in Italy." He indicated some of these criminals communicated with one another, but there was no formal organization. Similarly, Palma acknowledged some Black Handers in Detroit knew extortionists in Chicago and the criminals exchanged techniques and gossip, but there was no national structure in place uniting the gangsters.

Between media sensationalism and finger-pointing within the community, it became difficult to disentangle extortion schemes from other criminal activities in the colony. Eventually, the term "Black Hand" became the dominant signifier for almost every crime committed in the Italian sector. Any shooting, stabbing or robbery that occurred in the neighborhood was a suspected Black Hand crime. Father Boschi offered some insight into the complexity of the situation. Referring to Black Handers, he said, "Whether they are members of the Mafia, I cannot say." Boschi claimed that Italy's government had been chasing Mafiosi out of the country and some of these men ended up in Detroit. Still, he argued the Black Hand letter scheme did not match the mafia's modus operandi. "There is in no case vendetta, no ranking grudge. It seems to be solely and simply a money-extortion graft," he added.

Tragically, it took a brutal murder to shed light on the nuances of crime in the community. Clues surrounding the death of Manuelo Visconte revealed another conspiracy separate from the Black Hand. The mafia may not have been behind the extortion campaign; however, evidence suggested it still operated in Detroit and was ready to settle old scores when called upon.

CRIME WAVE

For the city of Detroit, 1908 was a record-setting violent year. The city recorded twenty-three homicides, an all-time high. Detroiters also experienced an increase in barroom shootings, physical assaults over monetary disputes, armed robberies, burglaries and domestic violence. As the year wound down, newspapers talked of "shocking crimes" and described how "a wave of violence [had] swept over the city." Other than Black Hand extortion schemes, however, few of these violent incidents seemed connected to organized criminal activities. The murder of Manuelo Visconte on October 24 was a notable exception.

When Visconte arrived at the hospital, he had a bullet hole in his liver and a slashed jugular vein. Earlier that evening, two men had broken into his apartment. One of the assailants grabbed his wife and started choking her. Awakened by his wife's cries for help, Visconte tried to fight off her attackers. One of the intruders put a revolver in the husband's stomach and pulled the trigger. The other intruder fired two additional shots at the victim. To finish him off, the two men started stabbing and slashing Visconte.

A relative living in the apartment ran for help, and the attackers left the scene. Visconte was still alive when he arrived at the hospital and gave a statement. He had $200 in the apartment and suspected the attack was a robbery. The police already had at least one suspect in mind. Detectives asked Visconte if he knew Salvatore D'Anna. Maneulo said he knew the suspect and described him "as a bad man." Still, the victim was unsure if D'Anna was one of his attackers. Visconte expired not long after giving his statement.

From the beginning, investigators did not believe the incident was a home burglary gone violently wrong. They believed the attackers were after Visconte, not his money. Because this was an Italian-on-Italian crime, there was a temptation to write this off as another Black Hand confrontation. The *Free Press* reported, however, that Police Chief McDonnell placed "no faith in the theory that any band of extortionists was responsible for the murder."

A few days later, the newspaper unequivocally stated, "In the Italian colony the murder of Manuelo Visconte is not attributed to the Black Hand gang." It turned out Visconte was a police officer back in Italy. One of his police investigations resulted in the conviction of an unidentified man who was sentenced to twenty years in prison. According to sources in the community, the convicted man's brother sought to avenge his brother by punishing the arresting police officer. Apparently, the brother had followed Visconte to Detroit, and his grudge was known in the colony. As a result, Visconte's family tried to buy their way out of the vendetta. They offered the man $100 in "blood money" but were rebuked. Only death could satisfy the brother's quest for vengeance.

It was not clear if the so-called brother *was* Salvatore D'Anna or if the "brother" simply asked for D'Anna's help. Either way, police investigators suspected him right away. As police gathered evidence, more information about D'Anna emerged in the press. Sources claimed he was the most feared man in the Italian colony. Importantly, it was clear he was not some Black

Hand crook. According to residents in the colony, D'Anna openly boasted of his connections to "secret societies." In fact, prominent members of the community did not go to the police when they needed protection from the Black Hand—they went to D'Anna. Apparently he held the police in open contempt and was known to carry "a revolver and stiletto" at all times, even though he did not have a gun permit. Reporters found it curious that Salvatore never held stable employment yet "was able to support his family in an almost luxurious style." By December, police felt they had enough evidence and arrested D'Anna, holding him without bail.

The arrest was actually one part of the Detroit Police Department's larger war on crime. In early December, the department promoted Louis Oldani to the rank of detective sergeant with much fanfare. Law enforcement hoped to launch a counterattack against crime in the Italian colony and needed a high-profile leader to head up a special anti-gang squad. Reporters described Oldani as "over six feet in stature, brave as a lion, and with wide experience." Residents of the Italian community had been pressuring public officials to appoint one of their own to a high-ranking position. Because of Oldani's familiarity with Italian language and culture, law enforcement and the community at large agreed he was the ideal man for the job.

Prior to the announcement, Oldani and the department had been keeping the special anti-crime unit a secret. To throw off suspected criminals, the department even staged a ruse where Oldani resigned from the force. Investigators hoped neighborhood gangs would let their guard down, thinking Oldani was no longer a cop. Even rank-and-file members of the department believed the resignation was legitimate. Meanwhile, Oldani quietly collected intelligence on a number of suspected Mafiosi. Detroit Police used this data as the primary intel for the new crime unit. "Oldani's work has placed in the hands of the police, the names, addresses and personal history of a number of Italians who have been looked upon with suspicion, but have never been investigated before," commented the *Detroit Free Press*.

On December 8, the anti-crime squad swept through the colony arresting dozens of suspects. According to reporters, the police offensive was "the first step in the dead-in-earnest campaign, a process of elimination, which will be followed by a constant 'tab' system on the members of Detroit's big colony, who manage to carry plenty of money, but are never known to do any work."

One of the higher-profile arrestees was none other than Francesco Paolo D'Anna—the community leader and sponsor of don Raffaele Palizzolo. D'Anna was well known in the community and instrumental

The Cinisi Terrasini train stop in Sicily as it looks today. The D'Anna family was from Terrasini. *Author's collection.*

to the formation of a Sicilian parish at Saints Peter and Paul Church. He was also a public notary and "steamship agent." D'Anna, in other words, coordinated immigration plans for members of the Italian colony.

According to investigators, there was another side to the public figure. Police alleged D'Anna was a fugitive from justice back in Italy. It turned out that D'Anna was a tax collector in Italy—but also a convicted embezzler. He was sentenced to pay a fine and serve a prison sentence just prior to his convenient arrival in Detroit. Oldani and his anti-crime unit arrested D'Anna and were especially interested in how the immigration agent "lived so well on so little." Oldani and his team failed to provide enough evidence to hold the suspect, but they sent a strong message across the colony. The anti-gang squad wasn't just chasing letter-writing extortionists; it was going to scrutinize the upper echelons of the community, too.

It wasn't long before the more notorious D'Anna was back in the headlines. The trial for the murder of Manuelo Visconte began in January 1909 and started off with high drama. During her testimony, Visconte's wife leaped from her chair and charged toward the defendant, screaming, "Brigand!" and "Assassin!" Meanwhile, the prosecution produced a witness who saw

Salvatore D'Anna wearing a hat and watch found at the crime scene. The defendant also had a scar on his hand; police claimed he sustained the injury during the attack on Visconte.

The defense team was well prepared and produced two crucial witnesses. Vito Bartolotti claimed he and D'Anna worked at Central Heating Company. More importantly, he testified that he saw D'Anna sustain the hand injury at work. Salvatore's wife took the stand and claimed she had never seen the hat and watch in her life. Critically, she claimed Salvatore was home sleeping the entire night of the Visconte murder anyhow. The jurors deliberated for only an hour and forty-five minutes before rendering a verdict: they found Salvatore D'Anna not guilty.

D'Anna was back on the street, and in the coming years, the streets of Detroit were about to get bloodier.

CHAPTER 3

DETROIT'S FIRST MAFIA WAR

W alter Langley warned his employer not to open the package. Langley worked in Vittorio Cusmano's pharmacy on Rivard Street. He told Cusmano the box was smeared with traces of gunpowder, but the pharmacist suggested it was graphite and continued tinkering with the package. Langley feared the worst and started walking toward the door when the parcel bomb exploded. The explosion blew out the plate-glass windows on both sides and tore through sections of the steel ceiling. The blast also hurled Langley and a sixteen-year-old delivery boy named Leo Ginsberg through the front windows and onto Rivard Street. One customer was injured, but Vittorio Cusmano and his associate Salvatore Cipriano caught the worst of the explosion. Cusmano was killed instantly, while the bomb tore off both of Cipriano's arms, blew out his abdomen and incinerated his face. Police and onlookers arrived and saw the spectacle of a bombed-out building. The scene was gruesome and disorderly. Fragments of body parts, medicine bottles, medical supplies, cigarette boxes and candies littered the storefront.

Police immediately suspected an underworld connection. Investigators identified Cipriano as a top man in the Giannola crime network. Meanwhile, a war had been waging for over a year in the Italian colony, and police rightfully determined the pharmacy bombing was another gangland hit. Newspaper articles described the killings as another example of feuding Black Hand gangs.

One letter to the editor, however, offered more insightful analysis. An Italian student studying in Detroit penned an op-ed for the *Detroit Free Press*.

The student explained that the recent gang warfare was a distinctly Sicilian situation. Do not confuse Sicilian gangs in Detroit with the Neopolitan *Camorra*, the author insisted. More importantly, the student dismissed the notion of a Black Hand operating in Detroit. According to the author, the war had nothing to do with extortion letters. The student explained, "The truth is there is no Black Hand in Detroit. There is only Mafia."

FROM COP TO *PADRONE*

The 1914 pharmacy bombing was part of an ongoing war in the Italian colony, and Ferdinand Palma was at the center of the conflict. Yet the famous detective's role in the conflict was not as an investigator. In fact, Palma was no longer a cop. Ironically, the former high-profile law enforcement officer was operating in the sketchy gray area between upperworld and underworld. He resigned from the department in 1905 and emerged as one of Detroit's most powerful *padroni*.

Italians used the term *padrone* to describe a particularly influential member of the ethnic community. The *padrone* had access to resources and was looked at as someone who could solve problems in the neighborhood. If you were looking for work, needed a loan or required someone with status to resolve a local dispute, you would go to the *padrone* (also referred to as "don") and ask for help.

Even as a police officer, Palma moonlighted as a private labor agent. For a fee, he would help Italian Detroiters find jobs in the construction and railroad industries. He also opened a bank and saloon. Palma had access to capital and rubbed elbows with influential non-Italians in Detroit. Therefore it was natural that he would emerge as one of the colony's most important dons. There were problems, however. Navigating through the corridors of power in both the Italian community and Detroit proper required dons like Ferdinand Palma to encounter unsavory elements of the city. Palma interacted with not only corrupt politicians and unscrupulous business owners but also people involved in the vice trades—gambling bosses, saloonkeepers, brothel owners and human traffickers. As a result, Palma found himself in legal trouble.

In 1905, the *Detroit Free Press* reported "one of the biggest wholesale frauds ever perpetrated in Michigan in connection with the manufacture of citizens, and that fully 7,000 foreigners, mostly Italians have thus [illegally] obtained papers inside the last three years." Newspapers identified Ferdinand

PALMA MUST FACE TRIAL

EX-DETECTIVE BOUND OVER TO RECORDER'S COURT.

CHARGE IS OBTAINING MONEY BY FALSE PRETENSES.

Case Will Be Brought on Soon at Request of Defendant.

Ferdinand Palma was the Little Sicily neighborhood's leading *padrone*. He was convicted of running an illegal immigration and voter fraud racket. *Author's collection.*

Palma as the head of the criminal conspiracy. Working with federal immigration officers, the Detroit Police Department issued arrest warrants for twenty-two individuals, including Palma. Though they suspected Palma had registered thousands of immigrants illegally, investigators were prepared to document 170 cases of fraudulent naturalization.

The illegal immigration scheme linked directly to allegations of voter fraud. Rumors of electoral fraud and voter intimidation circulated for years, but this was the first time law enforcement had launched a formal investigation. After expediting the naturalization process, Palma would quickly register the new citizens as voters. Palma promised citizenship, and in return the individual would vote according to the *padrone*'s direction. Here's how the scheme worked:

upon receiving his ballot, the new citizen would go to the city clerk and explain he could not read or write. Under the law, ignorant voters were to cast their ballots in an open booth. The voter would go to the open booth, and Palma's henchmen would be standing there to "assist" the new citizen.

Prior to the election, Palma would offer up his voting bloc to the highest bidder. And the corruption was bipartisan. In the most recent election, his henchmen instructed voters to cast ballots for the Democratic mayoral candidate and Republican presidential candidate. Italian voters testified before the grand jury that they never received any payment for their votes. In other words, all political payoffs went directly to the don.

Another local don emerged during the investigation and trial. Joe Moceri from Terrasini, Sicily, was linked to the immigration scheme. Investigators alleged Palma would go to Moceri and ask him to round up Italians for the naturalization scam. Another *padrone*, Moceri was known as the "King of the Italian Colony." Witnesses testified that the "King" would sign off as the official witness during the naturalization process at Detroit Recorder's Court. Moceri would verify that the individual had been in the United States for X amount of years. Investigators alleged Moceri would inflate the number of years so the person could be eligible to vote.

Moceri escaped any legal ramifications, but Palma faced twenty-one counts, including voter intimidation and extortion. He was convicted on only one count of falsifying documents. Palma was sentenced to one year in prison and up to a $1,000 fine. Detroiters in the Italian colony, however, predicted the don would not spend one day behind bars. They were right. Palma appealed, and the judge ordered him to pay the fine rather than spend time in prison. Meanwhile, the district attorney dropped all additional investigations.

The *padrone* avoided incarceration, yet seven years later, he faced a new round of challenges. On November 10, 1913, an assassin shot Palma with a sawed-off shotgun. The don was rushed to St. Mary's Hospital with sixteen slugs in his chest. Before he underwent surgery, police asked Palma about the shooting, but he would not cooperate. Instead, he told his interrogators not to worry: "If I live I'll get every one of them."

MAFIA RIVALS

The shooting of Ferdinand Palma was the latest in a tit-for-tat conflict beginning in 1911. Palma and Joe Moceri were not the only dons operating in the Italian colony. Other men like the Giannola brothers (Tony, Sam and Vito) were not only influential but also feared in the community. Like Moceri, the Giannolas were from Terassini, Sicily. The brothers actually settled in Ford City, a town twenty miles south of Detroit (located in the area known as "Downriver"). Yet their network of business and familial relationships extended deep into Detroit's Italian neighborhoods. The brothers invested in saloons, pool halls, pharmacies, grocery stores, ice trucks and restaurants. They weren't run-of-the-mill entrepreneurs, however. Most major players in the saloon and pool hall sectors were also involved in gambling and prostitution rackets. Extortion was another illegitimate tactic utilized by the brothers. If you were a restaurant owner or grocery store owner, the Giannolas expected you to buy your liquor, ice and produce from businesses inside their network. If not, you would find your store vandalized or even bombed. One scheme favored by the brothers was to steal supplies from a wholesaler and sell it back to the injured party. In 1911, police raided one of the Giannola grocery stores and found over $2,000 worth of stolen merchandise, including fourteen barrels of wine and three barrels of olive oil.

As the dons of Detroit accumulated wealth and status, their relationships with one another became more complicated. In some cases, there was a laissez faire policy, and in other situations, they collaborated. Still, at other times the dons clashed. The Adamo brothers (Vito and Salvatore), for example, established a fierce rivalry with the Giannola family. Like the Giannolas, the Adamo brothers had business investments Downriver and in Detroit. Both sets of brothers operated competing liquor stores in Ford City. The Giannolas had the additional benefit of owning an icehouse. To gain advantage over the competition, the brothers offered free ice with each liquor purchase. The tactic was successful and nearly put the Adamo store out of business.

Observers at the time traced the rivalry to the liquor store competition. It is important to note, however, that the Adamo brothers were invested in the same rackets as the Giannolas. Vito and Salvatore Adamo had extensive arrest records. Salvatore was known on the street as a top gunman. The truth was the two families were competing for control of Detroit's evolving mafia.

To injure their rivals, the Adamos targeted Giannola lieutenants operating in Detroit. The dangerous Salvatore D'Anna was the first target. D'Anna was a Giannola loyalist. He also hailed from Terrasini, Sicily, and the two families were related through marriage. In the summer of 1911, D'Anna, along with the Cassisi brothers (Carlo and Antonio), was shot while walking down Riopelle Street. Carlo was shot in the head and died instantly. Antonio, meanwhile, died at the hospital. Newspapers speculated that D'Anna would also die from his injuries and reported the Italian community was happy to be rid of the violent Mafioso. The speculations were premature, however, and D'Anna survived. As he recuperated, the police offered protection in return for his cooperation. Salvatore D'Anna just laughed. He knew he would be back on the streets soon enough and would handle things himself.

By wounding D'Anna and taking out the Cassisi brothers, the Adamo faction sent a powerful message. As a result, things cooled off, and it was almost two years before the rivalry turned bloody again.

All-Out War

It was the spring of 1913 when neighbors John Gervasi and William Catalano were shot to death in front of their Clinton Street homes. The initial suspects were the Cracchiolo brothers (Pietro and Giuseppe) from Carini, Sicily. Police identified the brothers as being involved in so-called Black Hand activities. Nevertheless, investigators realized this was not a simple extortion case. They did not believe this was a Black Hand incident but rather involved a "Sicilian Secret Society." According to informants, a contest was held, and the Cracchiolo brothers drew the shortest straws. As such, they were obligated to carry out the assassinations. The brothers were arrested, but powerful interests intervened and Gervasi's wife was offered money to withdraw her testimony against the brothers.

A few months later, another murder was linked to the Gervasi and Catalano shootings. Pietro Lamia was stabbed to death on June 1. Lamia was friends with Gervasi and Catalano. According to police informants, the Giannolas believed Lamia was going to tell law enforcement what he knew about the murders and had to be silenced.

The Adamo group responded by taking out the Giannola gang's top man in Detroit. Just before midnight on August 5, two gunmen walked up to Carlo Caleca and fired several shots point blank. Because the Giannolas lived in Ford City, they needed a street boss to run things up in Detroit. Carlo Caleca was their man. Observers described Carlo as the top underworld figure in Detroit at the time—"his pockets filled with money, his henchmen ready to do his bidding, he walked about the quarter and bragged about his power." He also had a reputation as the most feared man in the entire Italian colony.

Downtown Detroit, Gratiot Avenue and Broadway Street. The cross-section was near Detroit's Italian colony. *Walter P. Reuther Library.*

The Giannola street boss had multiple arrests and was the lead suspect in the throat-slashing murder of Joseph Trimmer. Caleca was also a top suspect in the murder of police officer Charles Schoof. The patrolman was shot in the head. Interestingly, unlike his contemporaries, Caleca was educated. Combining smarts with a violent streak, Caleca was the right man to oversee operations in Detroit.

Vito and Salvatore Adamo knew if they were going to make inroads in the Detroit underworld, they had to remove Caleca. In fact, to make sure it was done right, Vito Adamo would take part in the hit himself.

Four days after the Caleca shooting, Detroit Police arrested Vito Adamo and Felice Buccellato on murder charges. Linking Adamo with the Buccellato name was an interesting development. This demonstrated the Adamo brothers had formed their own alliances with powerful men of respect. Buccellato was one of the oldest mafia families in Castellammare Del Golfo, Sicily. Felice's brothers and cousins were important men of honor operating in Castellammare and Detroit.

According to police, Carlo Caleca identified Adamo and Buccellato as the assassins in three antemortem statements. When officers first arrived, Caleca told them, "I am dying. I am going to tell who the men are who shot me." Carlo told officers he had recognized Adamo and Buccellato at the corner store earlier that evening. He explained, "Yes, I am sure I knew them; I could not be deceived on them people, because I know them well." Caleca left the store and was walking down Russell Street with someone known only as "Joe from New York" when Adamo and Buccellato jumped out from the alley with revolvers aimed at the pair. Vito grabbed Caleca while Buccellato started shooting. Adamo fired shots as well. Carlo was shot twice in the leg and once in the abdomen and took a fourth bullet through his right ear. Joe from New York was hit in the leg.

As Caleca lay dying, police brought Adamo and Buccellato into the hospital room for another statement. Investigators asked him once again if these men were the shooters. The patient responded, "Take them away. They are the ones." At that point, Buccellato confronted the dying Caleca: "Look at me, look squarely at my face, don't look around the other way. Look at my face and tell me if I am the man, if I am one of them, or was there." The Detroit street boss could only sob, "I don't want to see them anymore; take them away."

Adamo and Buccellato went to trial for murder in October 1913. This was a high-profile case that captured the Italian colony's attention. One theory circulating was that the community had actually hired Adamo to kill Caleca. According to this argument, Adamo was the head of the "White Hand," a vigilante group hired to battle local gangsters. The prosecution even jumped on the theory and claimed the community paid Adamo and Buccellato $1,000 to remove Caleca from the neighborhood permanently. There is no proof that the White Hand actually existed, but it does seem that Adamo was a popular figure. Whereas Caleca was universally feared, Adamo had a group of supporters. During the trial, his cell was decorated daily with fresh flowers delivered by admirers in the neighborhood. Either way, the prosecution's case fell apart when people close to Carlo Caleca, including his wife, testified that he didn't recognize his attackers. Adamo and Buccellato were acquitted.

In September, before the trial even started, two gunmen ambushed Tony Giannola. Fortunately for Giannola, he escaped with minor injuries. Two weeks later, the Giannolas tried to exact revenge in one of Detroit's earliest examples of a drive-by shooting. Vito Adamo and his brother Salvatore were walking near the corner of Hastings and Fort Streets when a "taxi cab with curtains drawn" drove up to them and opened fire. Vito and Salvatore survived, but three bystanders were wounded. Police immediately suspected the Giannola brothers. The cops arrested Tony Giannola, but he negotiated a lesser charge of carrying a concealed weapon.

Meanwhile, the Giannolas were busy reorganizing the Detroit operation now that Caleca was gone. Four days after Caleca's funeral, the Giannola gang met to strategize and pick a new street boss. Unsurprisingly, they picked the veteran Mafioso Salvatore D'Anna.

Ferdinand Palma was next on the hit list. Ignazio Galante was a cashier working at Palma's bank when he heard a loud noise. Galante thought one of the big bookcases had tipped over. He walked back into the offices to inspect the noise when he saw Ferdinand Palma stumbling through the hallway with a chest full of shotgun-blast wounds. Galante called the police immediately, and Palma was taken to St. Mary's Hospital. Sixteen slugs tore through the *padrone's* chest, and one of his hands was so mangled that doctors had to amputate two his fingers. Palma was confident he would survive and told the police, "I don't know anything about it, and I'm not going to die anyhow."

Police suspected Palma was caught up in the Adamo-Giannola war, but to figure out who pulled the trigger, they needed to determine which faction the *padrone* supported. Until they sorted that out, the police simply arrested members of both factions. They arrested both Adamo brothers and two members of the Giannola gang: Salvatore Cipriano and Joeseph Stefani. Still not sure which side ordered the hit, one thing was clear: the hit was so brazen that it must have been orchestrated to send a public message. Until this point, most gangland slayings were midnight alley attacks, but this was a hit on a public figure in a public place during business hours. But what exactly was the message?

Solving the puzzle was difficult because Palma was known to associate with both factions. For example, he was close with top Adamo supporter and prominent beer baron Pietro Mirabile. Palma also strongly supported Adamo and Felice Buccellato during their murder trial. The *padrone* acted as the official translator and adviser for the defense team. According to the newspapers, Palma "exerted considerable influence in their trial." But Palma also had connections to the Giannola group. When Giannola lieutenant Salvatore Cipriano was arrested on charges of horse stealing, Palma furnished the $2,000 bail. And whenever Detroit Police picked up Tony Giannola, Palma arrived to negotiate a release.

Just six days later, police were investigating another shooting. Filippo Lacolla was known in the community as Ferdinand Palma's "straw-boss." In other words, he was the unofficial supervisor of Palma's other henchmen. Lacolla was having drinks and shooting pool with friends when four gunmen barged into the pool hall and starting shooting. Lacolla was hit in the shoulder but survived the attack.

Three days later, another Palma associate was assaulted. John Belchia was shot three times with a sawed-off shotgun. Belchia survived the shooting, and police had a suspect. Investigators were looking for a familiar face: Salvatore D'Anna. Police announced that the well-known Mafioso was also a lead suspect in the Palma and Lacolla shootings. This time, investigators had a cooperating witness: Filippo Lacolla. With Lacolla's sworn statement, police issued an arrest warrant for D'Anna.

With these developments, the circumstances surrounding the Palma attack were becoming clearer. If D'Anna was behind the three shootings, then it was likely the Giannolas ordered the hits. While the Giannolas had friendly dealings with Palma in the past, from their perspective, the *padrone* was ultimately in the Adamo camp. In order to completely take over Detroit, the Giannola brothers needed to neutralize the Adamo support network.

The Adamo brothers were feeling the heat. According to newspaper descriptions, "the brothers went to their work in fear and trembling. They never left each other's side, and as they walked along the street they peered on all sides." Unfortunately for the brothers, they were not cautious enough.

Four days before Thanksgiving, two gunmen ambushed the Adamo brothers on Mullet Street. Vito and Salvatore were riding home in one of Pietro Mirabile's beer wagons when two shadowy figures jumped out from the alley and unloaded their shotguns. Vito and Salvatore were lying dead in the gutter by the time police arrived on the scene. The hit was well orchestrated. Police officer Glenn Brown usually patrolled that section of the neighborhood, but each day between 4:30 and 6:00 p.m., Brown left his beat to direct traffic at Mack Avenue and Mt. Elliot Street.

Meanwhile, rumors circulated throughout the community that the war was not over. Remnants of the Adamo faction were plotting counterattacks. Police strongly suspected Adamo loyalists were planning to assassinate the top two Giannola lieutenants: Cipriano and D'Anna. In fact, the Giannola street boss was still locked up for the Lacolla shooting, and cops believed that police custody was the only thing keeping D'Anna alive. As for the Giannola gang members, they were plotting more executions. Adamo benefactor and booze baron Pietro Mirabile and Ferdinand's brother Alfred Palma were top on the hit list.

Both Palma brothers and Mirabile were being extra cautious. Mirabile did not travel anywhere without at least two bodyguards. Ferdinand Palma actually left the city to recuperate in an undisclosed location. Both men did make public appearances at the Adamo brothers' funeral on Thanksgiving Day. Later that afternoon, the two dons held a private conference to reevaluate Detroit's underworld situation.

TWO SICILIANS SLAIN IN ITALIAN COLONY OF DETROIT; FEUD RESULT

Sawed-off Shotgun Used by Slayers of Vito and Salvatore Adamo, Brothers

The Adamo brothers were frequently front-page news. *Author's collection.*

In the meantime, the Giannola faction scored another victory when Filippo Lacolla backed away from his testimony against D'Anna. Lacolla claimed the whole thing was a misunderstanding. The Giannola gang also tried to take out Adamo supporters Leo Pagalino and Nicola Dedona. Pagalino was shot point blank, and Dedona's grocery store was bombed. Both men survived. One week earlier, someone had set fire to Salvatore D'Anna's stable, killing his horse. D'Anna ran a fish-peddling operation, so this was a calculated move to hurt his business. Nevertheless, it seemed the Giannola faction had secured victory.

Yet by the spring of 1914, Adamo loyalists were ready to launch one last counteroffensive.

BOMBING CAMPAIGN

Leo Ginsberg was standing in front of the post office when two men of Italian descent approached him with a request. They gave him a fifty-cent piece and instructions to deliver a package. Ginsberg's memory was a bit fuzzy, but he thought the package was addressed to "Antonio Giannola." It turned out there was no address that exactly matched the package. So Ginsberg tried to deliver the box to a residential home that almost synced with the address. The resident was not expecting any deliveries but nevertheless helped the young man. He saw the name on the package and instructed Ginsberg to try Tony Giannola's liquor store on Lafayette Boulevard. Giannola owned a liquor store located next door to the Cusmano pharmacy. Salvatore Cipriano was at the Giannola store when Ginsberg arrived. The Giannola henchman wasn't sure what to make of the box, so he told the delivery boy to follow him next door to the drugstore. Cipriano was suspicious and asked Vittorio Cusmano if he suspected the item was a package bomb. The druggist started tinkering with the parcel and ended up triggering the explosion.

Newspaper accounts described how the bomb was constructed: "Inside the box were four or five sticks of dynamite, side by side. On top of the explosive was some loose powder, with slugs or bullets. Sandpaper in a sliding cover of the box was arranged so that it would ignite matches when the cover was moved." Law enforcement believed Cipriano and Tony Giannola were the bomb targets and that Cusmano was collateral damage.

Investigators immediately targeted the city's remaining Adamo supporters. Detroit Police raided multiple locations, including the Buccellato boardinghouse and Adamo grocery store, owned by Vito Adamo's widow. Fifty suspects were arrested altogether. Journalists noted that four suspects stood out: Felice Buccellato, his cousin Antonio Buccellato, Buccellato associate Liborio Diliberti and Vito Adamo's brother-in-law Salvatore Polito. The *Detroit Free Press* described Felice and Antonio Buccellato as particularly "important prisoners."

A few months earlier, Felice had been arrested for suspicious behavior. Police received a tip that Buccellato was walking up and down the neighborhood carrying a sawed-off shotgun. According to informants, he was seeking out an unidentified target. This was not the first time police received such a tip. By the time police arrived, Felice was back at his grocery store, but police took him to the precinct for questioning.

After the bombing, the Buccellatos were under scrutiny again. During the boardinghouse raid, police confiscated shotguns and ammunition. Leo Ginsberg stated that Antonio Buccellato "strongly resembled" one of the men who ordered the package delivery. According to newspaper accounts, Antonio kept his cool, and "Buccellato did not appear in the least concerned by the boy's statements."

Police determined the bombing was only the latest plot against the Giannola group. On at least two occasions, Liborio Diliberti ordered wine for his restaurant from the Giannolas. The cops believed each order was an attempt to ambush the brothers. Tony and Sam Giannola, however, never traveled in Detroit without at least eight bodyguards, with Cipriano acting as head of security. As a result, the Adamo faction had to devise alternative methods.

To put the plot in motion, the Adamo group consulted with New York mobsters. It was known throughout the Detroit underworld that New

Yorkers specialized in package bombs. Nick Dedona arranged for two New Yorkers to arrive and brought them to Diliberti's restaurant for a meeting with the Adamo leadership. The New Yorkers also visited the Buccellato boardinghouse.

Killing Cipriano was a huge move for the opposition, but overall the counterattack failed. First of all, the Giannola brothers remained uninjured and continued business as usual. Second, the public killing of a civilian like Vittorio Cusmano angered the Italian colony and actually generated sympathy for the Giannola group. The funeral for Cipriano and Cusmano was the largest memorial service in the history of Detroit's Italian community. Over one thousand people marched in a procession that included ninety-one funeral carriages. Over five thousand people attended the funeral. Ferdinand Palma even came out of hiding to attend the services. Such a public display sent a message that he did not sanction the bombing and in all likelihood had shifted his support to the Giannola side.

Finally, the bombing produced a heightened level of police scrutiny. Investigators were unable to solve the bombing, but they had enough evidence to hold the suspects on other charges. In an interesting development, family and friends of the arrestees negotiated a deal with the police. The support group brought gifts and food to the police asking them to release the prisoners and, in exchange, guaranteed the suspects would leave Detroit for good. Law enforcement agreed and gave the remaining prisoners until April 24, 1914, to vacate the city. The exiled group included Felice Buccellato, Antonio Buccellato, Liborio Diliberti and Salvatore Polito. Even Vito Adamo's wife left for Sicily, never to return.

The Adamos were gone, but the Buccellato clan members maintained a strong presence in the city. And in three years, they would find themselves at the center of Detroit's murder zone.

CHAPTER 4

MURDER ZONE

Harold Roughley was used to dangerous situations. As a veteran of the Detroit Police Department, Roughley battled with local hoodlums on numerous occasions. He also fought the Germans as a soldier of fortune during World War I. During one incident, Roughley engaged an enemy spy in hand-to-hand combat. Back in Detroit, chasing dangerous murder suspects was part of the job. Early on Monday morning, May 5, 1919, Roughley and three other officers tracked down local gangster Louis Caruso to his home on Clinton Street. Detroit Police were quite familiar with Caruso, a suspected bootlegger and auto thief. Now Caruso was a suspect in a double homicide case only a few hours old. Roughley knocked on the door several times, but there was no answer. Officers at the scene asked a neighbor to knock on the door, and finally a woman from inside yelled out that her husband was not home. Roughley wasn't convinced and asked his fellow officers to stand back as he prepared to knock down the door. As he started smashing his way into the house, Caruso fired his double-barreled shotgun, blowing a hole through Roughley's chest. The shotgun blast proved fatal, and the decorated officer received a hero's funeral.

For the average Detroiter, Roughley's killing signified an all-too-common occurrence inside the city. Gang-related killings were frequent, and police were occasionally caught in the crossfire. What investigators failed to realize was that Roughley was collateral damage in a transatlantic mafia war started decades earlier. The intrepid police officer was investigating Caruso for the double murder of Giuseppe Buccellato and Mike Maltisi. It is likely that Roughley suspected the killings were connected to a local turf battle. In actuality, a clan war involving the Buccellato family had reignited in Western Sicily, and the feud spread across the Atlantic to Detroit. The blood feud started in Castellammare Del Golfo, but now the vendetta was producing bodies inside the murder zone.

BROTHERS IN BLOOD

Detroit newspapers covered the Roughley killing and linked the case to the Buccellato and Maltisi murders. Reporters, however, overlooked an important detail: Giuseppe Buccellato was the younger brother of Adamo gang ally Felice Buccellato. As noted in the previous chapter, the Detroit Police Department had banished Felice and his cousin Antonio Buccellato

BLACK·HANDERS GET BUCCELATO

Grocer Arrested in Cipriano Bomb Case, Killed in Vendetta.

Believed To Have Been in Plot To Slay Bartender, That Failed.

Felice Buccellato's murder was a major news story. *Author's collection.*

from Detroit as result of the Cipriano and Cusmano bombings in 1914. The Buccellatos kept a low profile for a few years, but in fact, they never left the area. Felice was lying low and relocated to Highland Park, a city inside the geographic boundaries of Detroit.

On Sunday, March 18, 1917, the name Felice Buccellato was back in the headlines. The night before, unknown parties lured Buccellato to his old neighborhood. It is unclear what convinced Felice to leave his Highland Park sanctuary, but he left to meet someone near his old grocery store. When he arrived at the corner of Orleans Street and East Lafayette Street, three gunmen ambushed Buccellato. Armed with revolvers, the assassins hit their victim at least six times, with a kill shot through the heart. There was a beat cop in the area who heard the shots. The officer noticed three gunmen running down an alley between East Lafayette Street and Monroe Avenue. He ordered the suspects to stop and fired two shots, but the men got away unharmed.

By Sunday morning, newspapers were speculating on the reasons behind the Buccellato hit. Reporters reminded readers that the Buccellatos were the main suspects in the Cipriano bombing. According to one theory, the Giannola gang finally exacted revenge for the Cipriano execution. As a result, Felice Buccellato was the latest casualty of an ongoing feud between "East Side foreigners." Still, another article acknowledged the rumor that this particular murder wasn't a local gang killing but rather had its origins in Sicily. Police arrested a handful of suspects, but the charges were dismissed before going to court. The Buccellato family would be in the headlines again soon, but in the meantime, the city still wrestled with the overall problem of gang violence.

THE HOMICIDE BELT

The year 1917 was a bloody one on the streets of Detroit. Newspapers situated the Felice Buccellato crime scene in the "heart of the murder zone." Journalists also referred to the area as "the homicide belt." Felice was already the fifth Detroiter gunned down in the neighborhood. On January 7, Giuseppe Caladrino from the Rosina Romail incident was shot near St. Aubin Street. Police investigators never produced any suspects, and the crime was never solved.

Vito Licata was the next body to fall. On Saturday night, January 28, two men shot Licata eight times in front of Ferdinand Palma's bank at Russell

Street and Monroe Avenue. As Licata crossed Monroe Avenue, two gunmen rushed out of Joseph Mason's Saloon and opened fire, hitting the victim five times in the upper body. The assailants then pointed their guns at surrounding bystanders and warned, "Get back or we'll blow your brains out." Licata was a well-known local gangster whose picture adorned the Detroit Police Department's Rogues Gallery. He was a suspect in several extortion cases but never prosecuted. Police managed to get Licata to Receiving Hospital, but the injuries were fatal. Adhering to the code of the streets, Licata refused to provide police with any information before he died.

Black Hand Squad detective Emmanuel Roggers had his own ideas about who killed Licata. On February 21, Roggers issued a warrant for the arrest of Tony Giannola. Roggers found proof that Giannola had purchased eleven firearms from a Toledo hardware store prior to the Licata homicide. More importantly, Roggers was able to match one of the guns found at the crime scene to the Toledo gun purchase. Authorities arrested Giannola, but he paid his $20,000 bail (a staggering amount in 1917). Despite the evidence gained from scientific policing, the case fizzled out, and Giannola walked.

The summer ushered in more underworld violence, but one murder stood out as particularly brazen and shocked even the most desensitized citizens. Anti-crime crusader and popular police sergeant Emmanuel Roggers battled Detroit's gangs for almost two decades. Roggers was a veteran of the Spanish-American War and joined the Detroit Police Department in 1901. He made detective in 1911 and was appointed head of the city's Black Hand Squad. According to his fellow officers, Roggers wasn't afraid of anything. Detroit's gangs, however, feared the detective greatly. Roggers was fearless, incorruptible and, because he spoke Italian, had a knack for developing gangland informants. By the summer of 1917, the underworld wanted Roggers out of the way permanently.

Late on Tuesday night, July 24, Roggers and fellow police sergeants Joseph Kolb and John Crowe were investigating a week-old murder that had occurred on Russell Street near Congress. The officers were particularly interested in surveiling a couple poolrooms on Lafayette. Both establishments were known gang hangouts. Throughout the night, Roggers and his squad observed a handful of underworld suspects, including Andrea Licata, Dick Caparotta and Antonio Russo, consorting in a squirrely way. Roggers told his officers, "They must be up to something," and the squad started tailing the trio. Darting in and out of alleys, the suspects were able to dodge their pursuers for a brief time.

Still walking down Lafayette, the officers were surprised to see Russo drive up next to them in a brand-new car. Suspecting the vehicle was stolen,

Roggers asked, "Where did you find such a nice car?" Russo told the cops he bought it legitimately from a guy on Belle Isle and could prove it if they wanted to take a ride. Taking him up on the offer, Roggers, Kolb and Crowe began entering the vehicle when at least two gunmen ran out of a nearby poolroom and started shooting. Detective Kolb was hit six times yet was able to fire three shots in return. Even an innocent bystander took a bullet in the cheek. Roggers, however, was hit the worst. The assassins hit him with twelve bullets, including multiple shots to the head, with one shot blowing out his left eye.

Sergeant Crowe was still in one piece following the ambush and chased after the fleeing gunmen. Crowe and other Detroit law enforcement conducted house-to-house searches well into early Wednesday morning. By Thursday, they had thirteen suspects in custody. Investigators started with Caparotta and Licata. They found five automatic pistols during the raid on Caparotta's house. Meanwhile, they dragged Licata down to Receiving Hospital to confront the wounded Joseph Kolb. Lying in his hospital bed, Kolb saw Licata's face and started shouting, "You dirty murderer, you shot poor 'Rog' and me, and you know it!"

Police arrested a number of other suspects, including former Detroit Police detective Thomas Balone. Sources on the street reported Balone had a vendetta against Roggers. Earlier, Balone had been kicked off the force and blamed Roggers for the demotion. Investigators also arrested Vincenzo "Jimmy" Renda and his brother Vito Renda, both seasoned members of the Giannola gang. Detroit Police even sent agents down to Wyandotte to arrest Sam and Vito Giannola.

Investigators ultimately settled on Andrea Licata and Jimmy Renda as the likely triggermen. Authorities initially held them without bail. Attorney Louis Colombo alleged the men were beaten while in custody and accused the department of police brutality. Eventually, the judge granted Licata and Renda bail at $20,000 a piece. Antonino Zerilli, Giovanni Vitale, Pietro Mirabile and Sam Viviano arrived and secured their friends' release. During the trial, the prosecution had not only Detective Kolb's testimonial but also the eyewitness accounts of Patrolmen Arthur Sommerville and James Orr. The officers were nearby when the shooting began and claimed they watched Licata and Renda wielding revolvers as they fled the murder scene. Nevertheless, the jury could not come to a consensus, and both men were released.

As for Emmanuel Roggers, he was given a military funeral and buried at Mt. Olivet Cemetery. Almost one thousand mourners showed up to pay their respects. Ironically, underworld lawyer Louis Colombo sang "Thy Will Be Done" as a tribute.

The Roggers murder reignited citywide conversations about the Sicilian community and related topics like immigration, assimilation and to what extent crime was wound up in these social issues. The day after Roggers's murder, newspaper headlines read, "Sicilian Reign of Terror." In August, the *Detroit Free Press* issued a special report on the Italian community titled "Fear Holds Little Sicily." The report offered a mixed assessment of the Italian quarter. Observers noted a vibrant social atmosphere filled with music and playfulness. Yet the report's main concern was the growing crime wave sweeping the area. In this regard, the report was a condemnation. The *Free Press* observed "unsanitary living conditions" everywhere and used the term "human hives" to describe residential neighborhoods. According to the article, the area was littered with "vile smelling saloons and poolrooms." It also portrayed residents as paranoid, apathetic and standoffish to non-Italians. More provocatively, though, the essay racialized the problem by referring to "dark-skinned Italians" and lamenting that these "swarthy" foreigners had taken over neighborhoods once inhabited by the great pioneering families of Detroit. The report concluded that the community was "a hotbed of crime and the haven of the choicest brands of thugs and cutthroats Detroit [had] ever known."

Despite increased police efforts, gangland violence continued, and near the end of 1917, the murder zone claimed one more life. This last homicide connected to the Felice Buccellato killing. The case ended up producing headline-grabbing courtroom drama and highlighted the international nature of Detroit's underworld.

Pietro Buccellato and his cousins battled rival families in Castellammare Del Golfo and Detroit. *Author's collection.*

ANGEL OF DEATH

By the end of 1917, Pietro Buccellato was a thirty-four-year-old Sicilian immigrant with a wife and three children. He left Sicily in 1912 and, like scores of other Europeans, sailed for the United States. Pietro's ship landed in Boston. His cousin Antonio Buccellato from Detroit was there to greet him. Pietro initially settled in Williamsburg, Brooklyn. Williamsburg was known as a colony for recent arrivals from Castellammare Del Golfo. Around 1914, Pietro and his family relocated to Detroit seeking work in the auto industry. His uncle Vincenzo Buccellato and several first cousins already lived in the Motor City, so it was a natural fit. By December 1917, Pietro was working at the Ford Plant in Highland Park and was looking forward to spending Christmas with his family. Decembers in Detroit were quite different than in his native Castellammare del Golfo. Although temperatures were cool during the winter months in Sicily, Pietro would have never experienced such harsh weather prior to settling in Detroit.

Pietro lived on Chene Street, located on the outskirts of Detroit's Italian section. Six days a week at 5:30 a.m., he walked to nearby Waterloo Street to catch the streetcar headed for Ford's assembly plant in nearby Highland Park. At such an early hour, the sky still gave the appearance of night. Each morning, Pietro stood under the street lamp and, like thousands of other Italians in Detroit, waited for the ride to social mobility.

Around 6:10 a.m. on December 22, Pietro boarded the streetcar when two men emerged out of the darkness with revolvers and started firing. Pietro shouted in agony and dropped his lunch. The assassins continued shooting and hit him ten times with steel jacket bullets. As the shooters took off running, Pietro stumbled over to an alley near Waterloo Street.

It did not take long for a police wagon filled with detectives to arrive at Chene and Waterloo. Remarkably, Pietro was still clinging to life. Detective Louis Oldani had replaced the slain Emmanuel Roggers as head of the Black Hand Squad and was in charge of the crime scene. Oldani recognized Pietro from the neighborhood. He asked Pietro if he knew the shooters. Newspapers at the time reported that Buccellato identified his killer as Giovanni Torres, but that was not accurate. All he stated was that it was "the same man that shot my cousin." This triggered Oldani's memory, and he recalled speaking to Pietro on the night of Felice Buccellato's murder. Pietro was taken to Receiving Hospital and died from his wounds shortly after.

Initially, investigators zeroed in on two suspects: Vincenzo Ilado and Joseph Brucia. It turned out that before relocating to Detroit, Pietro had lived near Ilado and Brucia in Brooklyn, New York. All three immigrants were from Castellammare del Golfo and were related to one another through a network of marriages. Once investigators realized the familial connections, they released the suspects and turned their attention to other New Yorkers.

By March 1918, Detroit Police had focused on Giovanni Torres and John Vultaggio as the primary suspects. Only nineteen years old, Torres was born in Palermo but was living in Manhattan. Vultaggio was thirty-three years old and from Castellammare del Golfo. He immigrated to the United States in 1908 and lived in Detroit for a few years. Both men were linked to the Schiro gang in Brooklyn. Though not Castellammarese himself, Nicolo Schiro headed a gang composed primarily of Mafiosi from the Sicilian coastal town. Investigators believed Torres and Vultaggio acted as hit men for the gang. Word on the street was that Torres earned $500 per hit. Police suspected he had killed as many as twenty people in locations ranging from Palermo and New York to Flint and Detroit.

Investigators also picked up solid information regarding motive. Police recognized Torres was imported as a hired executioner, and the Pietro Buccellato murder transcended local gang warfare. Instead, it seemed likely that Buccellato was the victim of a blood feud extending from Sicily to Detroit. According to one report, Pietro uttered in his last breath: "They're going to kill us all." At the time, Detroit Police were more interested in finding the suspects and proving their guilt than disentangling the origins of a Sicilian vendetta.

Police also suspected Torres had mistakenly killed two innocent bystanders in pursuit of Buccellato. Joe Constantine was shot on December 8, 1917, at the same streetcar stop as Buccellato. Constantine survived, but Paul Mutoc was shot to death on December 18 at the same corner. Investigators noted that both men bore a strong resemblance to Pietro.

Interestingly, by the time Detroit issued an arrest warrant, Torres was already being held by the New York police on unrelated charges. He was a suspect in an armed robbery case that ultimately fell apart. The teenage Torres already had a notable criminal resume. Not only was he a murder suspect in his native Palermo, but in the States he was also arrested for assault in 1916 and robbery in 1917. Initially, New York was reluctant to extradite Torres to Michigan. Detroit detectives sent telegrams to New York urging their colleagues to expedite the process. They feared Torres would flee back to Sicily if New York refused extradition.

Detectives secured their suspect, and Torres arrived in Detroit on March 26. News reporters noted how "dapper" and "cherubic" the alleged

Attorney Louis Colombo seated on the far left. He represented Vito Adamo, Felice Buccellato and Giovanni Torres, among other prominent Mafiosi. *Walter P. Reuther Library.*

professional hit man looked. The press dubbed him "Angel Face." Police tried to take a statement, but Torres claimed he did not understand English. Investigators did have an eyewitness, though. Joseph Collins, a laborer at the Dodge Brothers Assembly Plant in Hamtramck, was waiting for a streetcar and stood only a few feet away from Pietro Buccellato at the time of the murder. Collins picked Torres out of a lineup, and legal proceedings were set in motion. The prosecution faced a familiar and challenging adversary as Torres secured Louis Colombo as his defense attorney.

Fortunately for Torres, Colombo obtained an adjournment for the trial. The defense claimed it needed more time to bring in alibi witnesses from New York. By June, the trial was underway again. Torres's wife was the primary witness for the defense. Colombo described her innocently enough to the jury "as the little girl in blue." Mrs. Torres spoke perfect English and testified that her husband worked in a New York wine shop owned by her father. She claimed Giovanni was working with her father on December 22, 1917. Furthermore, Torres told the court that August 1917 was the last time he was in Detroit. Colombo also picked apart eyewitness Joseph Collins. The defense attorney prompted Collins to admit he had an arrest record. He also cast doubt on Collins's reliability as a witness considering how dark the early morning was on December 22. Lastly, Colombo highlighted the fact that Torres and Buccellato did not know each other. Colombo connected this to an "absence of malice" defense. Ultimately, the defense produced enough reasonable doubt, and the jury voted to acquit.

Judge Charles Wilkins presided over the case. Wilkins was a former assistant U.S. district attorney and traced his genealogy to founding father and Declaration of Independence signee George Ross. The veteran recorder was outraged by the jury's verdict of not guilty. Wilkins stated this was an "outrageous miscarriage of justice." According to the judge, there was enough evidence to not only convict Torres of the Pietro Buccellato murder but implicate him in the Felice Buccellato murder as well. Witnesses testified they saw Torres in the neighborhood around the time of Felice's execution. "This is the first miscarriage of justice in my court, and I hope it will be the last," commented Wilkins. The judge pointed out that everyone who testified that on Torres's behalf was a blood relative or related by marriage. He added, "I don't know what protection the people are going to have from bandits and assassins if jurors are going to be swayed by such testimony as was brought by the defense in this case." Wilkins also lamented that Torres was the third mafia gunman charged with murder and acquitted in the last month.

Detroit's Police Department was disappointed as well and took action. Detectives immediately rearrested Torres on immigration charges. Lieutenant William Good wanted to deport Torres to Italy to face murder charges. Torres was only sixteen at the time of the alleged killing. Detroit reached out to investigators in Italy, hoping they would request extradition for the "Angel Face" killer. In the meantime, Torres was released on bond and waited for his deportation hearing. Lieutenant Good argued that the Italian community in Detroit had little faith in law enforcement and that's why bringing Torres to justice was so important. Ultimately, the Angel of Death survived another round of legal proceedings and was back on the streets of New York.

Unable to convict Torres, Judge Wilkins had one more card to play. A few days after the verdict, Wilkins announced he was firing the twelve jurors. He sent the names of all twelve men to the Wayne County Jury Commission and informed the commission that each man was unfit to serve the court system in future cases. This action agitated some of the jurors. One fired back, "I suppose [Wilkins] wants the jurors to come out and consult him before they vote." Another member commented that he was grateful the Sixth Amendment was in place to protect defendants from overreaching judges. Colombo also jumped in and defended the trial-by-jury system. Furthermore, he issued a statement claiming, "I give my word of honor that Torres did not kill Buccellato." Wilkins, however, was not swayed and was convinced the verdict sent the wrong message to local gangsters.

The Buccellato murder trial generated front-page news in Detroit. Until this point, most shootings were unsolved. To arrest and bring an alleged murderer to trial was a rarity. There were other sensationalistic components of the story. First, Torres challenged the existing stereotype of the mafia or Black Hand gangster. Instead of a rough-and-tumble immigrant bandit, Torres was a handsome and suave teenager. Second, the trial featured a murder victim with a prominent underworld last name. Lastly, the international and New York elements of the investigation added a cosmopolitan flavor to the case.

Less than a year later, another member of the Buccellato family would be killed. This time, the murder set off a chain of events resulting in the death of Officer Harold Roughley.

THE LAST BUCCELLATO

Giuseppe Buccellato buried his brother Felice in an unmarked grave on March 20, 1917. Nine months later, he buried his first cousin Pietro Buccellato. Felice and Pietro rest at Mt. Olivet Cemetery in Detroit.

Knowing he was a marked man, Giuseppe took his family outside the homicide belt. They moved to Newport Avenue, located in a relatively newer neighborhood six miles northeast of Little Sicily. Giuseppe immigrated to the United States when he was thirteen years old. Like most Buccellatos in America, he lived in New York for a brief period. Around 1910, his Uncle Vincenzo told him the Buccellato family was moving to Detroit in pursuit of economic opportunity. Giuseppe followed along and soon married. Giuseppe did not stay in the Motor City long. He relocated to Port Huron and, alongside other Italian immigrants, worked in the salt mines.

Eventually, Giuseppe moved back to Detroit to work in one of the automotive factories. But there were other economic opportunities in the big city. By 1913, his brother Felice and cousin Antonio Buccellato were working with the Adamo gang. Like other gangland figures, the

Buccellatos were involved in bootlegging. Even though alcohol was legal, you could sell bootleg liquor at a cheaper rate and undercut the price of legitimate alcohol manufacturers.

Today's descendents of the Buccellato family remember hearing childhood stories about the Buccellatos meeting and mingling with fellow bootleggers like the Purple Gang. Historically this is unlikely considering the Purple Gang did not establish itself as an underworld powerbroker until the mid-1920s. This does not mean the Buccellato family stories were inaccurate. During the height of their power, the Purple Gang was so infamous that the very term "Purple Gang" served as a universal signifier for any Detroit gangster. Crime historians William Helmer and Rick Mattix describe this phenomenon: "By the time these stories saw print any criminal from the Detroit area was automatically labeled a member of the Purples." It is likely that Buccellato family members heard stories about relatives meeting with other Italian bootleggers and, in the fog of popular vernacular, included the Purple Gang as part of the story.

Michigan politicians granted Detroit's bootlegging community a huge opportunity when, on November 7, 1916, they implemented a statewide ban on the sale of alcohol. The ban went into effect on May 1, 1918. The Buccellatos, among others, were eager to capitalize on the huge demand for contraband booze. Before Prohibition, the family operated a saloon on Russell Street in the heart of the Italian neighborhood. Once state prohibition set in, they changed the name of the establishment from a saloon to a "soft drink emporium." Of course, police suspected the "soft-drink" bar was still selling booze. On May 23, 1919, Detective Robert Ellison entered the emporium and claimed Joseph Buccellato (Antonio's brother, not to be confused with their cousin Giuseppe Buccellato) gave him a product sample. Ellison took it to the department for chemical analysis. The bottle tested out at 49.96 percent alcohol—about 100 proof. Joseph Buccellato was arrested for violating Prohibition law and charged with a $300 fine. This was a steep fine in 1919 but a small price to pay compared to the millions made selling illegal beer and liquor.

At thirty-two years old, Giuseppe Buccellato had to balance the lure of bootlegging profit with the reality that someone was gunning for him. He hoped that by moving to Newport Avenue, his family was a safe distance from the murder zone.

On May 4, 1919, Giuseppe's wife and children left the house to visit with nearby relatives for a baby shower. Later that afternoon, the otherwise peaceful neighborhood was interrupted by the sounds of gunshots. With all the commotion, Giuseppe's wife decided to return to Newport Avenue. As she

Giuseppe Buccellato and his wife. Giuseppe's brothers and cousins fought the Magaddino clan in Detroit and Sicily. *Author's collection.*

walked into the house, she was horrified to find the bullet-ridden bodies of her husband and their twenty-eight-year-old roommate, Mike Maltisi. Ordering the children to hide in the closet, she checked the house for intruders. Soon police arrived and recorded statements from witnesses. Neighbors saw three men between the ages of thirty and forty walk into the house and seconds later heard gunshots. Witnesses saw the same men run out of the Buccellato house. At the crime scene, police noted that the gunmen fired off seven shots. Giuseppe and Maltisi died instantly.

Investigators gave the standard explanation that Buccellato and Maltisi were victims of a Black Hand feud. The police were familiar with both victims. They knew Giuseppe was related to the recently deceased Pietro Buccellato. And the Black Hand Squad had arrested Maltisi in the past as a murder suspect. According to Buccellato relatives, Maltisi was an innocent bystander. They claimed he was saving up money and hoped to return to his wife in Italy. Going by this theory, Maltisi was murdered to eliminate any witnesses to the Buccellato killing   wrong place at that wrong time. We will probably never know if Maltisi was a target or collateral damage, but police described the crime scene as if Buccellato and his roommate were preparing for war. Inside the flat they found several sawed-off shotguns, a number of automatic pistols and boxes of ammunition.

Either way, police hoped to find the killers, and veteran patrolman Harold Roughley was on the case. Roughley was known on the streets as the "Kid Policeman" because of his boyish looks and youthful demeanor. Still, criminals knew not to underestimate the young patrolman. He had a reputation for toughness and transgressing the legal boundaries of appropriate police behavior.

A few years earlier, Roughley had resigned from the force and embarked on a career as a soldier of fortune. Upon American entry into World War I, he tried to enlist in the army, but the military would not take him due to poor eyesight. Instead, he joined the transportation corps and served in Mexico before joining the Young Men's Christian Association. Through his YMCA affiliation, Roughley ended up in Italy. There he worked as a trainer for the Italian army and was decorated by the government for bravery.

His command of the Italian language served him well once he relocated to Detroit. Back in the Motor City, Roughley's resignation from the police department was withdrawn, and he rejoined the force. Because of his familiarity with Italian language and culture, the department assigned him to the Black Hand Squad.

On the morning of May 5, Roughley and three additional officers were investigating the double homicide of Giuseppe Buccellato and Mike Maltisi. Louis Caruso was the main suspect at the time. Roughley traced the getaway car used by the assassins to a garage in Toledo. According to a witness, the car was left there by "three Italians." According to the Michigan Registry, the vehicle was registered under Caruso's name. The suspect had a checkered past. Police identified him as a member of local gangster Pietro Bosco's auto theft ring. In 1910, he was arrested for writing Black Hand letters and in 1911 for possession of dynamite. Later he was arrested in Port Huron for stealing horses and served time at Marquette Prison. On May 5, he added cop killing to his criminal resume.

After watching Caruso blast a hole through Roughley's chest with a double-barreled shotgun, the other officers retreated and sent for reinforcements. Fellow Black Hand Squad officers Louis Oldani and William Good arrived at the scene. Caruso had barricaded himself and would not stand down. After an hour-long standoff, Oldani tried another tactic. He was friendly with Louis's uncle Philip Caruso and convinced the uncle to intervene. Philip negotiated with his nephew, and Caruso surrendered. Inside the house, police confiscated the twelve-gauge shotgun murder weapon, an automatic pistol and nineteen quarts of whiskey. Caruso, meanwhile, claimed he never heard the officers announce themselves as police. He stated he thought they were "enemies sent to kill him."

Caruso was in trouble for the Roughley killing, but in terms of the Buccellato homicide, the case started to fall apart. It turned out the vehicle in question was not the getaway car after all. Caruso actually sold the vehicle five months before the Buccellato killing, and it should no longer have been registered in his name. Furthermore, the Toledo suspects linked to the car ended up being Hungarian, not Italian. Caruso was no longer a suspect in the Buccellato and Maltisi double murder.

Eventually police arrested a handful of new suspects, including Leonardo Cadili and Tony Ruggirello. Cadili lived at the Buccellato house and was related to the Ruggirello family through marriage. Lacking evidence, the charges against Cadili and the others were dropped, and the case went cold.

Nevertheless, there was significant and intriguing information inside Detroit Police Department File No. 181 regarding the Giuseppe Buccellato murder. According to the file, Officer Kramer received a call from Giuseppe's wife the day after the murder. She stated that her husband was murdered by the following people: Vito Bonventre, Stefano Magaddino and Mariano Galante. Bonventre, Magaddino and Galante were from Castellammare Del Golfo and affiliated with the Schiro gang in Brooklyn. The men resided in New York and addresses were provided, but Detroit investigators did not follow the lead. Later, Officer Kramer communicated with Mrs. Buccellato and asked her about the allegations. Interestingly, she denied making such a call and claimed "she never heard of the subject." Officer Kramer reported that she was "very cooperative and appeared to be telling the truth." As a result, Detroit investigators felt this was a dead lead.

The case generated interest again two years later when fishermen stumbled upon the body of Camillo Caiozzo in Tucker's Cove, New Jersey. Caiozzo was from Castellammare. Police investigators began to see the connections between Castellammare del Golfo and Mafiosi operating in America. It turned out the Buccellato murders in Detroit and the Caiozzo murder were part of the same Sicilian blood feud. Investigators realized Detroit was a battleground in an epic transatlantic mafia war that changed the complexity of organized crime in America.

CHAPTER 5

VENDETTA

In August 1921, Camillo Caiozzo was in the New Jersey coastal town of Neptune City to negotiate a business investment. Specifically, Caiozzo wanted to invest in the prostitution rackets. He was scheduled to meet with a local Jersey pimp by the name of Salvatore Rose. The pimp's real name was Salvatore Cieravo, and he ran a brothel that fronted as a hotel. Caiozzo's childhood friend Bartolo Fontana was there to broker the deal. The two friends were hanging out at Cieravo's farm when Camillo noticed a shotgun. "Let's go duck hunting," Caiozzo suggested. Fontana agreed, and the two men took the shotgun out to a marshy and leafy section of town located near Shark River. Caiozzo was looking forward to a spending a leisurely afternoon of sport with his lifelong friend. Fontana had other ideas.

They were deep in the woods when Fontana aimed the shotgun at his friend's back and squeezed the trigger, blowing a hole through Caiozzo.

Around ten days later, crabbers uncovered Caiozzo's roped and weighted body in Tucker's Cove—a location four miles from the mouth of Shark River. Soon investigators linked the murder to Bartolo Fontana. It did not take long before the suspect started talking. Investigators had uncovered a murder case with international implications. According to Fontana, there was a mafia war waging in Sicily, and it had spread to the United States. As a result, bodies were piling up in New York, New Jersey and Detroit.

The murder and Fontana's subsequent confession produced a national media sensation. Journalists noted there was one commonality that linked the feuding gangs: "All the murderers came from the little town of Castellammare Del Golfo."

FORTRESS BY THE SEA

Castellammare is a charming Sicilian fishing village located forty miles west of Palermo. Today it is a developing town and popular location for tourists. Castellammare's most famous landmark is an ancient castle that sits on a peninsula overlooking the Tyrrhenian Sea. The castle is the town's namesake—Castellammare translates to "Castle by the Sea." Restaurants and shops line both sides of the castle's promontory. The marina curves to the west of the castle, and there fishermen come and go as they have for generations.

Castellammare del Golfo also has a noteworthy history. The ancient Greek city of Segesta used the Gulf of Castellammare as a strategically

The famous castle by the sea in Castellammare del Golfo. *Author's collection.*

important harbor. Centuries later, Carthaginians used the port to transport wheat to the Roman Empire. Yet it was under Arab rule that the location evolved into a proper town. Arab rulers expanded agricultural activities in the area, cultivating vines, olive trees, almond trees and fruit trees.

Eventually, Norman invaders conquered Sicily, and throughout the centuries, the town passed from one imperial power to another. From the Kingdom of Aragon to the Houses of Bourbon and Savoy, monarchies fought for control of Sicily. Due to its location, Castellammare remained a significant trade port under each regime.

By the 1500s, the town had expanded, adding churches and increasing its population. Meanwhile, local fishermen developed sophisticated techniques for trapping tuna. During the mid-1800s, Castellammare played an important role in the struggle for an independent Sicily.

Despite its idyllic beauty and distinguished history, by the late 1800s and early 1900s, the town had developed an unsavory reputation. During the 1950s, writer Gavin Maxwell observed widespread illiteracy, poverty and malnourishment in the coastal village. Maxwell wrote, "Castellammare has an evil reputation in Sicily." According to the writer, the town was steeped in "blood and violence." During the course of his visit, Maxwell was able to diagnose the cause of such plight. He wrote, "While this is due partly to poverty, desperation, and traditionally Sicilian methods of vengeance, the chief cause is that the district is under control of the mafia."

ORIGINS OF A MAFIA CLAN

Bartolo Fontana and Camillo Caiozzo were born in Castellammare del Golfo. Fontana told investigators the Caiozzo murder was part of a larger conspiracy involving other Castellammaresi. He identified the following men as part of the plot: Vito Bonventre, Stefano Magaddino, Bartolommeo DiGregorio, Francesco Puma, Mariano Galante and Giuseppe Lombardi. Fontana said the men belonged to a gang known as the "Good Killers." The press loved the name and speculated the Good Killers were involved in over one hundred homicides. Men like Bonventre and Magaddino were known gangsters living in Brooklyn, New York. As a result, journalists suspected the murders were connected to the bootlegging and illegal gambling rackets. The *Detroit Free Press*, however, noted another possible angle. Based on Fontana's testimonials, some of the killings were part of a vendetta originating in

Sicily. Rather than fighting over gangland turf, the killings were "the result of personal feuds and of feuds handed down from father to son."

This analysis started to make sense once Fontana identified other victims. Fontana claimed the hit squad targeted Sicilians in Detroit as part of the grudge. Based on his testimonials, the *Detroit Free Press* reported the Good Killers were connected to the "Buccellato feudist gang." The paper was referring to the unsolved murders of Felice, Giuseppe and Pietro Buccellato. According to Fontana, several years earlier, the Buccellatos had killed a member of the Bonventre family in Brooklyn. The Buccellatos allegedly sawed the victim into pieces and placed Bonventre's body in an oven. Based on Sicilian notions of honor, such a depraved act demanded retribution. According to this theory, Vito Bonventre formed the Good Killers to exact revenge on the Buccellato family.

Fontana correctly tied the Good Killers to the Detroit Buccellato murders, but the true story was more complicated than a tale about a hacked-up body in a Brooklyn oven. The Bonventre and Magaddino clans were at war with the Buccellatos, and while the exact origins of the conflict are unclear, the fighting began in Castellammare.

To better understand the blood feud, it is important to describe the economic and political conditions that produced such powerful mafia families. During the early 1800s, Sicily belonged to the Bourbon dynasty based in Naples. Under the feudal arrangement, barons and lords rarely lived in smaller towns and villages. Nobles tended to live near urban centers like Palermo. Approximately twelve aristocratic families owned most of the land in Castellammare. Because the barons spent most of their time in Palermo and Naples, they were absentee landowners. This created an economic opportunity for middlemen to govern the land. For example, noble families hired *gabelloti* to manage their estates. *Gabelloti* were peasants and in some cases small landowners who enjoyed reputations as local strongmen. The *gabelloto* was an entrepreneur, however, and not interested in working the land. He would sublet parts of the estate to smaller farmers. The small farmer would have to buy grain and other supplies from the *gabelloto*, usually with high interest. Estate managers also hired *campieri* as enforcers. The *campieri* were usually friends and relatives of the *gabelloto*. They collected debts and taxes and protected property from local bandits. In many cases, *gabelloti* mismanaged the estates on purpose in order to drive the baron into debt. Not wanting to bother with uncultivated land, the noble might sell the land to his estate manager. Accumulating property was important because it presented the

Castellammare marina as it looks today. *Author's collection.*

rare opportunity for social mobility. Overall, these conditions produced political turmoil on the island.

During the 1840s, the land around Castellammare was fertile for growing Sumac, wheat, grapes and olives. There were sheep and cattle ranches, too. Yet the peasants were starving. The *gabelotti* also controlled access to fresh water. The local population grew to eleven thousand people, yet the large estates were deliberately scaling back grain production. Big landowners made a fortune by creating scarcity but produced a hunger crisis in the village.

The political arrangement was untenable, and Sicilians revolted against the Bourbon dynasty in 1848. Castellammare del Golfo played an important role in the rebellion. A variety of interests coalesced to start the insurrection. Urbane patriots desired Sicilian independence, while peasants clamored for economic justice. In Castellammare, families like the Buccellatos financed the revolt.

The formation of the mafia was entwined in these events. Secret societies flourished during such precarious times. Freemasonry greatly influenced the urban intellectuals clamoring for insurrection. Radical political groups adopted secret rituals and blood oaths and carried out clandestine activities.

VICE, CORRUPTION AND THE RISE OF THE MAFIA

Eventually, these trends seeped into the Sicilian countryside and coastal towns like Castellammare. Local strongmen, like the *gabelotti* and *campieri*, had accumulated wealth, property and status. Soon they formed their own secret societies, complete with ceremonies and secretive classifications that resembled those of the freemasons and liberal revolutionaries. Members of these rural secret societies did not name their organizations. They simply referred to themselves as men of respect. Italian journalists and law enforcement, however, used one word to describe such groups: mafia.

Influential families in Castellammare did not support the revolt for ideological reasons. They saw political revolution as a business opportunity. While large families were expanding their holdings, Bourbon lords and the clergy still owned most prime real estate. If Sicily were to drive the Bourbons out, mafia clans were situated perfectly to expropriate feudal lands.

The revolt of 1848 was unsuccessful, yet the mafia proved to be a politically slippery target. Even though they supported the rebellion, mafia leaders negotiated a deal with the Bourbon regime. In exchange for leniency, the powerful clans would restore order in the countryside. In other words, the mafia would crack down on banditry and neutralize any remaining subversives. Plus, as a practical manner, the barons still needed the *gabelotti* and *campieri* to manage the feudal estates and administer local governments.

Sicily experienced another rebellion in 1860. This time the revolt was successful. Sicilian rebels did not achieve total independence, though. Instead, the Italian patriot Giuseppe Garibaldi negotiated an alliance with the northern Italian Kingdom of Sardinia. As a result, the unified nation of Italy was born.

Initially, the residents of Castellammare were enthusiastic about joining a unified Italian state. Peasants and small farmers, however, soon realized that promises of land reform and democratic equality were unlikely to be fulfilled. Castellammarese rebels launched another revolt in 1862. The rebels were an eclectic group that featured peasants and Sicilian rebels fighting alongside Bourbon sympathizers and conservative clergymen. This time the mafia sided with the new regime, and the insurrection was put down.

Just as planned, once the Bourbons left, lands were auctioned off and prominent Mafiosi bought up new properties. Such families emerged as the bourgeoisie of Castellammare—wealthy, respected and politically connected. Court documents from 1864 identify Giuseppe Buccellato as one of the original Mafiosi in the area (the Giuseppe Buccellato in Detroit was his nephew). It would not be long before his nephews were engaged in open warfare with rival families.

BLOOD FEUD

Buccellato was a ubiquitous name in Castellammare. The first Buccellato likely settled in Castellammare during the late 1400s/early 1500s. Because the clan was large, with many family trees, let alone branches, other prominent families like the Magaddino and Bonventre clans intermarried to strengthen their positions. The Magaddinos and Bonventres also intermarried with the wealthy Bonanno family. United, the Magaddino/Bonventre/Bonanno alliance proved a formidable foe for the Buccellatos.

Sorting out the genealogy is vital to understanding mafia politics. The brothers Stefano and Giuseppe Magaddino ruled the Magaddino clan (their nephew in Brooklyn was also named Stefano). Their sister Carmela Magaddino married Martino Bonventre. They had a daughter named Caterina, who married Salvatore Bonanno. Salvatore's brother Giuseppe was an important member of the clan as well.

The tri-family alliance owned vast amounts of land. Like that of other wealthy families, their land produced olives, figs, tomatoes, grapes and wheat. The families owned livestock as well. By subletting land to small farmers, large families like the Magaddino clan held great influence over the local peasantry. As a result, residents viewed great landowning families as the true authority in Castellammare.

With access to wealth and clout, mafia clans developed important political networks. Through these connections, the Magaddinos and others were able to secure government-funded projects in Castellammare. Such projects put people to work and deepened the mafia's powerbase. Mafiosi also required local merchants to pay a monthly tribute. The tribute was a euphemism for extortion. It was a type of tax one paid for the privilege of operating a business on mafia territory. Tribute payments did, however, guarantee protection from bandits, swindlers and other petty criminals. Meanwhile, families like the Bonannos specialized in smuggling horses and other livestock from North Africa.

Castellammare was an active port town, so the dons received a cut of the action along the piers. And there was a lot of money to be made by controlling access to the harbor. Scores of Sicilians were immigrating to the United States. Consequently, there was huge demand in America for goods like prosciutto and olive oil—goods transported from port towns like Castellammare. Because of the money to be made in land, livestock, extortion rackets, smuggling and government contracts, the competition among families was fierce.

Magaddino Alliance

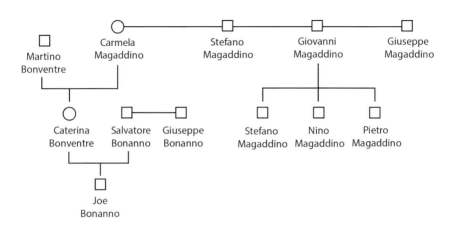

Magaddino alliance family tree. *Author's collection.*

The competition for resources shaped the collective mindset of the Castellammarese families. Sicilians experienced centuries of subjugation and impoverishment. From the Mafioso's perspective, land accumulation, government contacts and controlling access to resources were the keys to social mobility. Because of the harsh realities of scarcity, Mafiosi viewed social mobility as a zero-sum game. If your family was enjoying prosperity, it came at the expense of mine. Ultimately, the Buccellatos viewed the Magaddino, Bonventre and Bonanno alliance as a provocation.

In terms of action on the pier, the Buccellatos suspected the Magaddino alliance was encroaching on their territory and vice versa. And each family accused the other of cattle-rustling. American godfather Joe Bonanno compared the situation in Castellammare to the conditions that produced conflicts in the American frontier. He wrote, "In the countryside behind Castellammare, there was not enough good grazing land. Ranchers, could not afford to fence in their property, so they had to let their cattle feed on common pasture used by other ranchers. These conditions almost invited rustling, and thefts of cattle resulted in retaliations."

Before fighting could begin, Stefano Magaddino and Giuseppe Bonanno were arrested and sentenced to home confinement on an island off the coast of Sicily. At this time, Felice Buccellato sat at the head of the Buccellato clan (the Felice Buccellato in Detroit was his first cousin). He had influence over the local constabulary and court system. Naturally, the Magaddino alliance suspected Felice orchestrated the house arrest.

Before long, Giuseppe Bonanno returned to Castellammare, and the Buccellatos decided to eliminate him forever. Bonanno was awakened one evening by one of his caretakers. The employee claimed he needed Giuseppe's help reining in some horses fighting in the stable. When the master of the house walked outside, he was greeted with a shotgun blast. Giuseppe Bonanno was dead.

Salvatore Bonanno felt obligated to avenge his brother's murder. Salvatore was actually studying to join the priesthood. The death of his brother, however, presented an existential crisis. He decided to leave the seminary and return to Castellammare. Once home, he took his brother's place in the Magaddino alliance. Joe Bonanno, in his autobiography *Man of Honor*, states, "Not long after Salvatore Bonanno returned home, two members of the Buccellato clan met their death."

After returning home, Salvatore cemented his bond with the Magaddino alliance by marrying Caterina Bonventre. Their son Joseph was born in 1905. Now a husband and a father, Salvatore Bonanno did not foresee living the life of a mafia warrior. He asked the Magaddino brothers if there was a way to negotiate peace with the Buccellato clan. Many years later, Giuseppe Magaddino recounted the story to his nephew Bill Bonanno. Bill recorded some of the details in his autobiography *Bound by Honor*. Giuseppe Magaddino argued that killing the Buccellato family chief was the only way out of the conflict. "Cut off the head of the snake…kill Felice Buccellato himself," suggested Magaddino. Salvatore bravely responded, "But I was taught that a good father brings peace to his family, not blood." Instead of plotting more violence, Salvatore asked Felice to act as godfather to his newborn baby. As Magaddino told the story: "Salvatore walked to the café with no bodyguards (and unarmed) and approached Felice Buccellato, asking him to be godfather to his son." The Buccellato don responded affirmatively: "I would be proud and honored to be the godfather of your son." The baby Bonanno was championed the "dove of peace."

After securing the peace, Salvatore took his new family and departed for America. The restless Bonanno wanted to raise his family somewhere beyond the provincial constraints of Castellammare. Once in America, the Bonannos settled in the Williamsburg neighborhood of Brooklyn, New York. Williamsburg hosted a large Castellammarese enclave and was the natural location for Bonanno.

Back in Castellammare, without the peacemaking Bonanno there to mediate, tensions between the factions continued to escalate. If either family experienced an unfortunate event, the other family suspected foul play immediately. According to Joe Bonanno, "If the Bonannos did not find a natural explanation for an event, they blamed the Buccellatos, and vice versa."

Meanwhile, the Magaddinos still pined for the death of Felice Buccellato. Giuseppe Magaddino recalled, "You know everyday Buccellato went to a café in the town square with his bodyguards and sat there like he was a king or potentate. He thought he was invulnerable—but he was not. I knew how to get to him."

Suspecting war was imminent, the Magaddino alliance summoned Salvatore Bonanno back to Sicily. Bonanno's presence once again had a calming effect on the factions, and the truce remained unbroken.

Bonanno, however, was called on to fight in another war: World War I. In 1915, Salvatore was drafted by the Italian army. He suffered injuries during a battle on the Austrian border. Bonanno returned to Sicily to recuperate but died from his injuries shortly after.

With the peacemaking Bonanno out of the way, the killings recommenced. On July 13, 1916, the Magaddinos shot to death Giovanni Buccellato. Nino Magaddino was the likely shooter. Nino was the nephew of Stefano and Giuseppe Magaddino. According to FBI documents, Nino was arrested in Castellammare for homicide on August 14, 1916. He was released for lack of evidence but later "denounced for robbery, rape and extortion."

Giovanni's brother Francesco was an important member of the Buccellato clan. Francesco demanded blood for blood and targeted Nino's brother Pietro. One week later, Francesco avenged his brother Giovanni by shooting to death Pietro Magaddino. The Magaddino clan leader Stefano was also attacked but survived the ambush. Francesco had an accomplice during the shooting. His aide was none other than Camillo Caiozzo.

THE GOOD KILLERS

Naturally, the Magaddinos sought retribution, but Francesco Buccellato and Caiozzo were elusive targets. If they couldn't kill Francesco, then his brothers would have to suffice. It turned out his elder brothers, Felice and Giuseppe Buccellato, lived in Detroit. Joe Bonanno commented, "The Magaddino family was not alone in having members in America; the Buccellato family did also. They were archenemies in Castellammare, and archenemies they remained in [America]."

The Magaddinos sent a cable to their nephew Stefano in Brooklyn. Stefano was the slain Pietro Magaddino's other brother. The cable instructed Stefano to take out the Buccellatos and their allies in Brooklyn and Detroit. On March 17, 1917, hit men from the Magaddino alliance arrived in Detroit and assassinated Felice Buccellato.

Felice's younger brother Giuseppe was honor bound to retaliate. Giuseppe and an unidentified accomplice traveled to Brooklyn to hunt down members of the Magaddino alliance. On November 11, 1917, they took out two Magaddino allies. Antonio Mazzara and Antonio DiBenedetto were shot to death on the corner of North Fifth and Roebling, in the heart of Williamsburg. Witnesses overheard four men arguing and the phrase, "If you don't tell us, we'll kill you." After the shootings, police found a guitar case nearby with two loaded double-barreled shotguns.

While in Brooklyn, the Buccellatos' hit squad tried to take out Stefano Magaddino and his right-hand man, Gaspare Milazzo. Gaspar was from Castellammare and a staunch supporter of the anti-Buccellato faction. The ambush was unsuccessful, and Magaddino plotted his revenge.

They targeted Frank Finazzo. Finazzo owned a pool hall in the Williamsburg neighborhood and was related to the Buccellatos through marriage. On the early morning of December 11, gunmen blew Finazzo's head off with shotgun blasts. Less than two weeks later, Giovanni "Angel Face" Torres and an accomplice traveled to Detroit and shot to death Finazzo's best friend and brother-in-law, Pietro Buccellato. Giuseppe Buccellato was able to lie low for a while, but on May 4, 1919, assassins killed him, too.

The Magaddino alliance managed to wipe out the core of Detroit's Buccellato faction. Yet more targets remained. For Stefano Magaddino of Brooklyn, eliminating Camillo Caiozzo was a personal matter.

Caiozzo managed to stay alive longer than the Detroit Buccellatos. He settled in Brooklyn and evaded his enemies for a few years, but the Magaddino alliance solved its problem when it ran into Bartolo Fontana. It knew Fontana was best friends with Caiozzo. According to Fontana, one day, three members of the so-called Good Killers gang cornered him in a Brooklyn hallway and pressed their pistols into his stomach. They demanded he kill his childhood pal or suffer the consequences. He knew if he didn't cooperate, he would be killed as well.

From the Magaddino perspective, Fontana was the perfect Judas. He had not only grown up with Caiozzo, but the Fontana and Buccellato families

Buccellato Clan

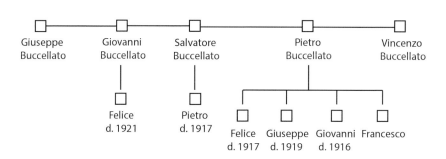

Buccellato clan family tree. *Author's collection.*

were also intermarried. As a result, Caiozzo would never suspect his friend of double-dealing.

During the summer of 1921, Fontana finally had the opportunity to carry out his deadly betrayal. He knew his friend recently made over $600 selling an embroidery business. Fontana suggested his friend invest the profits in the prostitution rackets. He told Caiozzo he would set up a meeting with a Jersey brothel owner named Salvatore Cieravo. They planned on staying at the brothel owner's farmhouse and spending the weekend in Neptune City. Meanwhile, Fontana informed Cieravo of his plans to do away with Caiozzo. Once at the farmhouse, Caiozzo unwittingly expedited his own execution by suggesting they go duck hunting. Fontana realized that would be the perfect opportunity to kill his unsuspecting friend.

After the shooting, Fontana returned to the farmhouse and informed Cieravo that the deed was done. The brothel owner was incensed when Fontana explained that he left the body right where it fell. Realizing they had to dispose of the evidence, Cieravo demanded they return to the scene of the crime. The two men dragged Caiozzo's body several feet and hid it under some brushwood.

Fontana and his accomplice returned and informed the Good Killers that the target was neutralized. Good Killers gang members Giuseppe Lombardi and Francesco Puma arrived in Neptune City not long after. The two seasoned gangland figures had more experience making bodies disappear. Fontana and Cieravo led them to the body, and the gang went to work. They pulled a sack over the man's head and tied twenty-five-pound stones around Caiozzo's neck and his knees. The gang of four finished the job by dumping the body in Shark River.

The Good Killers misjudged the river depth, and a few days later crabbers noticed something odd in the waters. Police arrived and discovered they had a murdered corpse on their hands. Investigators found an address in the man's coat pocket with the name Caiozzo. Equally important, they managed to connect the clothesline used to tie up the body to clothesline at the Cieravo farmhouse. Salvatore Cieravo was arrested on August 12.

Just as New Jersey investigators were getting started with Cieravo, Bartolo Fontana contacted the New York Police Department seeking protection. Fontana was not only guilt ridden by his actions but also sensed the Good Killers would eliminate him too. Fontana confessed the whole story to veteran detective Michael Fiaschetti. He provided details of the Caiozzo killing and implicated the Good Killers. The cooperating witness pointed out that each member of the gang was from Castellammare del Golfo. He explained how the Bonventre and Magaddino families had formed the hit squad and tasked it with eliminating the Buccellato family. According to Fontana, Vito Bonventre and Stefano Magaddino were the gang's leaders.

Fiaschetti believed the story and employed Fontana in a sting operation. As part of the ruse, Fontana contacted Magaddino and told him things were too hot in Brooklyn. He explained that he needed cash to flee the city. Fontana suggested they meet at Grand Central Station. Magaddino told him not to worry, that he would provide money and arrange a safe house in Buffalo. The gangster fell for it, and New York police detectives were waiting for him when he arrived at Grand Central. Magaddino protested and battled with the arresting officers. Ultimately, the suspect was beaten unconscious with police billy clubs.

Detectives also rounded up Vito Bonventre, Giuseppe Lombardi, Francesco Puma, Mariano Galante and Bartolommeo DiGregorio. The last perp was related to the Bonventres and Magaddinos through marriage.

Meanwhile, New York investigators decided to contact their colleagues in the Detroit Police Department. Not only had Fontana lived in Detroit for a time, but he also claimed the Good Killers were behind the unsolved Buccellato murders. Inspector William Good and Black Hand chief Bert McPherson traveled to New York to consult with Fiaschetti and interview Fontana. The Detroit detectives found the story compelling but also recognized an opportunity. Soon, Fontana's confessional started to expand.

No longer was the Good Killers case solely about a vendetta originating in Castellammare. Almost immediately, detectives started connecting the Good Killers to every unsolved Italian homicide in Detroit. And the yellow press ate it up. By some media accounts, the Good Killers were responsible for over 125 murders nationwide, including as many as 70 in Detroit alone. Local newspapers reported there was a mass grave located near 7 Mile Road and Gratiot. According to the press, the Good Killers used the land to bury dozens of victims.

While the media embraced such sensationalistic stories, the court system held a more sober view. Defense attorneys for Magaddino and his gang argued this was all a fantasy conjured up by Fontana. They argued Fontana had premeditated the murder of Caiozzo so he could rob him of his $600. The strategy worked, and prosecutors dropped the broader conspiracy case and instead focused on the four individuals present during the murder and subsequent cover-up.

Prior to the trial, another footnote to the Castellammarese blood feud emerged. While already being held for the Caiozzo murder, Francesco Puma was charged with another killing. Eight years earlier, Vito Buccellato had been stabbed to death in New York City. His body was found in the basement of an overcrowded tenement building. New evidence materialized, and in early September 1921, Puma was arrested.

Puma was able to secure a trial postponement and was back on the streets after posting $20,000 bail. Yet on November 4, 1922, his luck ran out. Puma was walking along East Eleventh Street in New York when a gunman crept up behind him and fired three shots. He died from his injuries. Word on the street was Puma had cooperated with authorities and had to be silenced.

As for his codefendants in the Caiozzo trial, Salvatore Cieravo was found not guilty. Giuseppe Lombardi was able to postpone his trial, and eventually prosecutors dropped the case altogether.

Bartolo Fontana was the only defendant found guilty. He served almost twenty years at New Jersey State Prison.

CODA

Vito Bonventre and Stefano Magaddino continued on as major gangland figures in New York. Vito became a top lieutenant in the Schiro crime organization, while Stefano emerged as the crime boss of Buffalo.

In 1921, Stefano's uncles in Sicily finally had their revenge on Felice Buccellato. Joe Bonanno explained, "There had been a funeral in town…for one of the Buccellatos. The coffin was kept closed. The man buried that day, I later found out, was Felice Buccellato. My godfather's body had been found in a gully. The body was in a burlap sack, hacked to death and too horrible to look at."

Francesco Buccellato captained the remnants of the clan but faced a new foe when Benito Mussolini took power in 1922. To escape the Fascists, Francesco, along with other Sicilian Mafiosi, fled to Tunisia.

Bartolo Fontana's confessions helped explain the Detroit Buccellato murders, but some of his story did not add up. He claimed the Good Killers traveled to Detroit to battle the infamous Giannola gang. The Giannola family, however, was from Terrasini and not concerned with the vendettas of Castellammare. Fontana was inaccurate, but back in Detroit the Giannola brothers did indeed fight a mafia war. They did not fight the Good Killers; they did, however, battle "Bloody" John Vitale for control of Detroit's lucrative rackets.

CHAPTER 6

BLOOD BROTHERS

Police labeled them the "Green Pepper Gang." Investigators received tips that a gang was smuggling booze into the city by concealing it under bushels of green peppers. To purchase the contraband liquor, customers used a special code. Ask for "extra hot peppers," and the gang sold you two bottles of whiskey hidden beneath each order. Agents with the Food and Drug Commission suspected the Giannola brothers were the masterminds behind the green pepper scheme. The commission identified the gang as one of the city's leading suppliers of illegal booze. Officers with the commission knew the brothers were also prominent in Detroit's produce industry. It was common to see the brothers selling fruit and vegetables at the open-air marketplace known as Eastern Market. So that's where investigators set up their sting operation.

On November 18, 1918, Sam Giannola and three companions entered Eastern Market with a truckload of peppers. Police ordered the driver to halt, but the truck sped off, traveling about a mile before law enforcement cornered the suspects. Officers aimed their revolvers at the vehicle and ordered everyone out. Examining the truck bed, police found forty-one barrels of liquor hidden beneath bushel baskets of green peppers. According to informants, the Giannolas had recently purchased eighty-six barrels of whiskey from a source in St. Louis. Investigators believed they uncovered some of that St. Louis whiskey in the pepper truck. Police arrested Sam Giannola and three members of the gang, including Giuseppe Braziola, Jimmy Renda and his cousin Tony Renda. The four men were charged with violating interstate commerce laws and selling illegal liquor.

The Green Pepper Gang used a similar truck to conceal booze. *Walter P. Reuther Library.*

The prohibition of alcohol changed the underworld in extraordinary ways. Profits from the booze business dwarfed the earnings one could make in other rackets. The Giannola gang emerged as the hegemonic power in Detroit's underworld and was on the verge of making a fortune through bootlegging. Complicating things, however, underlings in the gang similarly recognized the lucrative potential of the booze racket. Certain members of the gang believed the leadership represented a significant obstacle to profit sharing. And there was only one way to remove the obstacle: kill the Giannola brothers.

THE GIFT OF PROHIBITION

Michigan ratified the Eighteenth Amendment in the spring of 1919. The amendment banned the manufacture, sale, transportation and importation of intoxicating beverages. The law required an enforcement mechanism, so Congress passed the Volstead Act in the fall of 1919. President Woodrow Wilson vetoed the legislation, but the House and Senate were able to override the veto. Interestingly, the State of Michigan experimented with prohibition before the nation did. On November 7, 1916, Michigan approved a statewide amendment banning the sale of beer, liquor and wine. The amendment was scheduled to take effect on May 1, 1918.

Political organizations like the Anti-Saloon League led the charge to criminalize alcohol. Locally, the league led a coalition of powerful allies that included wealthy industrialists and prominent religious leaders. Midwestern capitalists like Henry Ford and Sebastian Spering Kresge financed the prohibition movement. Ford supported prohibition for social and economic reasons. Socially, he held a paternalistic worldview rooted in Christian theology. According to Ford, frugality and sobriety led the path to providence and grace. Economically, industrialists viewed prohibition as a way to increase worker productivity.

Such views complemented religious arguments for banning booze. Religious leaders claimed the sale and consumption of alcohol promoted sinful and idle lifestyles. In Michigan, this crystallized into a political critique of Detroit's saloon culture. According to critics, not only were citizens wasting time and money buying and consuming drinks at local taverns, but the saloon was also the nexus of vice in the city. Prohibitionists described the saloon as a hotbed of gambling, usury and prostitution. As a result, once Michigan adopted prohibition, politicians were not going to wait until the spring of 1918 to enforce dry laws. To expedite prohibition, the legislature passed the Damon Law in 1917. The legislation prohibited the importation and possession of liquor from other states. Michigan State Police and the Michigan Food and Drug Commission were assigned with enforcing the law.

Detroiters and other Michigan residents set up elaborate smuggling networks the moment prohibition laws went into effect. The Green Pepper Gang purchased its whiskey from St. Louis, yet most Detroiters smuggled booze from Ohio or across the border in Canada. The *Literary Digest* labeled this moment the "Great Booze Rush." Almost daily, the sixty miles of road between Toledo and Detroit was congested with thousands of automobiles trafficking whiskey. Dixie Highway linked the two cities, and locals referred to the highway as "Avenue de Booze." People also smuggled alcohol from Ohio on trains and trolleys and through riverways. Historian Philip Mason wrote, "According to Michigan Food and Drug Commission, more than

Detroiters line up to buy booze hours before state prohibition laws take effect. *Walter P. Reuther Library.*

800,000 quarts of whiskey were seized by police between May 10, 1917, and February 1918, mostly along the Dixie Highway."

Quite simply, Detroiters wanted to drink and were going to circumvent regulations designed to prevent them from doing so. Consequently, the price of alcohol shot up. According to Philip Mason, "A case of whiskey costing eight to ten dollars in Toledo sold for seventy-five dollars in Detroit." Such profit margins attracted members of the underworld. Soon local gangs added bootlegging to their criminal resumes. Italian gangs were not the only ones getting in on the action. In fact, in the early years of prohibition, non-Italian outfits like the Billingsley Brothers and the predominantly Jewish Oakland Sugar House Gang ran the strongest bootlegging operations. Underworld figures had the infrastructure to import large quantities of alcohol. The gangster bootlegger was not a small-time hustler, brewing beer in the basement to sell to neighbors or someone smuggling a couple bottles of whiskey for personal use. Already experienced in trafficking narcotics and stolen goods, gangs had access to sophisticated contraband networks. Gangs also had access to the manpower and trucks necessary to facilitate large-scale distribution operations. In some cases, they didn't have to smuggle alcohol at all. Gangster bootleggers set up industrial-sized stills to cook up booze locally.

As more and more gangsters became involved in bootlegging, it was inevitable that conflicts would occur. The Giannola gang was investing in the booze trade but was also involved in gambling, prostitution, extortion and larceny. There was a lot of money to be made, yet there was some discontent within the organization. Some members believed the bosses were taking home a disproportionate share of the illicit profits. The Giannola brothers became aware of such treacherous attitudes and decided to send a deadly message.

KILL THE KING

Even though the Giannola brothers were top gangland figures in Detroit, they lived in nearby Ford City (also known as Ford Village). Initially part of Ecorse Township, the city of Wyandotte annexed Ford City in 1922. Prior to annexation, the village was located north of Wyandotte and featured a substantial Italian population. Many immigrants settled in Ford City and nearby townships to work for the Michigan Alkali Company.

While most Italian immigrants led peaceful and productive lives, others like the Adamos and Giannolas thrived in the Ford City and Wyandotte underworlds. By the time prohibition was in full swing, Wyandotte was considered the third most corrupt city in the Detroit area. The Giannola brothers started off extorting local Italian businesses. Soon they organized illegal gambling enterprises like card, dice and numbers games. They even sold homebrewed beer years before prohibition. Hijacking and theft were lucrative rackets, too. Unsurprisingly, the brothers established a reputation for violence. Tony and Sam were arrested in 1912 for the murder of Ford City resident Salvatore Biondo. The victim was shot in the head, his body tied to a wagon and dragged through a field before finally being set on fire. Combining muscle with a lust for profit, it was only a matter of time before the brothers set their eyes on Detroit.

Because they lived outside the city, the brothers appointed a street boss to run things in Detroit. Initially, Carlo Caleca occupied that position. Salvatore D'Anna took over the role after Caleca's murder. By 1916, twenty-six-year-old Pietro "Peter" Bosco was the official Giannola viceroy in Detroit. Bosco was born in Castellammare del Golfo. Back in Sicily, the Bosco family

Families

Terrasini	Cinisi	
Bommarito	Badalamenti	Sicily
D'Anna	Palazzolo	
Giannola	Vitale	
Licavoli		
Moceri		
Tocco		
Zerilli		

By 1919, members of the two most powerful mafia factions tended to be from either Cinisi or Terrasini. *Author's collection.*

aligned itself with the Buccellato clan. In Detroit, however, there is no evidence that Peter Bosco worked with the Buccellatos. Instead, Peter was the consummate American gangster. Bosco was not interested in fighting old-world blood feuds; his main concern was making money. Like his bosses, he had a fearsome reputation. On January 17, 1916, he was arrested for the murder of Joseph Agosta. As he was dying, the victim identified Bosco as the shooter. Apparently, Agosta lent Bosco $200 and wanted it back. Earlier that day, Agosta had confronted the borrower, but Bosco refused to pay. Later that evening, Agosta was shot three times while walking near the corner of Mullett Street and St. Aubin Street. Bosco was the lead suspect and no stranger to run-ins with the law. He had been arrested several times and ran a crew of extortionists, kidnappers and auto thieves. Ultimately, Bosco beat the murder rap.

Peter continued running things in Detroit, but eventually there was tension between the street boss and the brothers. Bosco oversaw a number of lucrative rackets and was a violent gangster in his own right. One can imagine how he started to resent having to send so much of his earnings to mob bosses in Ford City. This is known in the underworld as "kicking up." Each mafia underling is expected to "kick up" a percentage of his earnings to the bosses. Tony Giannola became aware of Bosco's dissatisfaction and started to suspect the street boss was withholding money. Tony also heard rumors that Bosco was plotting a takeover. Giannola decided to strike first.

VICE, CORRUPTION AND THE RISE OF THE MAFIA

On October 9, 1918, Peter Bosco was shot to death in his headquarters. The Bosco Garage on Trumbull Avenue and Ash Street served as the gang's base of operations. Fifteen minutes before the shooting, two of Bosco's men entered the garage and conversed with the street boss. Investigators believed the same two men reentered the garage minutes later and executed their gang leader. Bosco inadvertently survived an earlier assassination attempt. Police confiscated his car and were looking for contraband when they realized the vehicle was rigged with explosives.

Tony Giannola hoped the murder would send a message to other subversives in the organization. In case there was any miscommunication, the brothers sent a few more messages.

Six days after the Bosco killing, the Messina brothers from Alcamo, Sicily, were gunned down. Mariano and Liborio Messina were walking on Mullet Street when two assassins ran out from an alley and shot the brothers several times in the head.

Three days later, the notorious gangster Joe Silver was shot to death. Silver was one of the few high-ranking non-Italians in the Giannola syndicate. Because he wasn't Italian, Silver could never be an inducted member of the mafia. Nevertheless, as a prolific criminal, he earned the Italians' respect. Silver was an international jewel thief and considered the foremost burglar in Detroit. Investigators suspected Silver led a crew of sophisticated thieves specializing in jewelry and furs. For his day job, he managed the Wyandotte Fruit Company, owned by the Giannola brothers. Law enforcement believed he functioned as the gang's bookkeeper as well. Once again, the Giannola brothers suspected one of their criminal associates was holding back. Joe Silver was likely responsible for a recent robbery that landed $50,000 worth of gems. It seemed the bosses were dissatisfied with their cut of the loot.

Silver was playing pinochle at three o'clock in the morning when he was summoned to a meeting. He left the game with mobster Louis Ricciardi. Silver was never seen alive again. Forensic evidence indicated the victim was shot while sitting in the front seat of a car. The notorious jewel thief was found with two bullet holes behind his ear. According to the autopsy, "one bullet severed his spinal column and the other lodged in the right side of his brain."

The Giannola brothers used violence to remind everyone that insubordination would not be tolerated. Tony Giannola, however, underestimated the numbers of disgruntled mafia soldiers in his midst. It was a fatal miscalculation.

EARLY ORGANIZED CRIME IN DETROIT

On January 4, 1919, newspaper headlines proclaimed, "King of the Sicilian Gangs Is Dead." Tony Giannola had been shot to death. The mob boss was attending funeral services for Giuseppe Braziola. The deceased man was a member of t
he Giannola organization. Braziola had been murdered, although the crime was unrelated to gangland activities. He got into an argument with his son-in-law, and the disagreement turned fatal. Tony Giannola arrived, not only to pay his respects but also to supply the funeral services with lobster, fish, fruit and bread. The forty-year-old mafia don stepped out of his car and walked toward the Braziola house on Rivard Street. Assassins waiting behind the house rushed out and ambushed the boss. Tony Giannola was shot in the head.

Even though gang violence was all too common in the Sicilian colony, the public execution of a major underworld figure like Giannola created a sensation in the community. Italian Detroiters rushed to the coroner's office to catch a glimpse of the infamous gang leader. Onlookers arrived to see a man stylish even in death. Lying on the slab, the don was impeccably dressed, still wearing his diamond pinky ring and diamond stickpin and with pockets full of cash. Journalists reported that although Tony Giannola was feared by many, some sectors of the Italian colony viewed him as a Robin Hood figure. Apparently the don gave generously to families in need and donated resources to religious and civic organizations within the Italian community. An elaborate funeral was held for the crime boss, but his brothers Sam and Vito did not attend for security purposes.

Back on the streets, Sam Giannola stepped up and took over as boss of the organization. As a result, he became a natural target for the rebel faction. Approximately one month after the murder of Tony Giannola, gunmen ambushed Sam Giannola and his brother-in-law Pasquale D'Anna. Giannola and D'Anna were arriving home around three o'clock in the morning when they were attacked. Giannola survived, but two bullets tore through D'Anna's chest, killing the brother-in-law. As with the killing of Tony Giannola, investigators believed the gunmen knew when and where their targets would arrive. Obviously the brothers were facing a well-organized plot to overthrow the regime. When reporters asked Sam about the situation, he said he knew who was behind the attacks. He added, "If I ever meet the man who killed my brother, I'll kill him."

BLOODY JOHN

Sam Giannola knew Giovanni Vitale was leading the opposition. Born in Cinisi, Sicily, Vitale moved to Detroit in 1913. He was known on the streets as "Bloody John." In addition to Vitale, the rebel group featured other members from Cinisi, including his brother Peter and their cousin Jim Vitale. Salvatore Palazzolo, Tony Badalamenti and Giuseppe Manzella were also part of the Cinisi crew. Badalamenti and Manzella were Bloody John's nephews. Being born in Cinisi was not a precondition for joining the rebellion. Vitale's right-hand man Salvatore Evola was from Palermo. The gang featured a number of Mafiosi from Alcamo, Sicily, including Salvatore "Singing Sam" Catalanotte, Santo Perrone and the Renda brothers (Jimmy and Vito). The veteran don Pietro Mirabile from Trapani, Sicily, also supported the uprising. John Vitale had been quietly supporting Peter Bosco's plans for regime change. Once Bosco was killed, Vitale realized it was only a matter of time before the Giannolas came after him. Ultimately, the hit on Tony Giannola was a preemptive one.

Police believed the rebel faction used Peter Vitale's grocery store in Ford City as its headquarters. Meanwhile, informants claimed Vitale was planning another attack on Sam Giannola. Three days after the D'Anna killing, county sheriffs visited the grocery store to ask about the wave of

Jim Vitale was a mafia soldier in the Cinisi faction. *Walter P. Reuther Library.*

violence. Expecting retaliation from the Giannola gang, the Vitale men were well armed and trigger happy. As sheriffs approached the store, the gangsters started shooting. A gunfight ensued, and Officer Joseph Burman was hit twice in the leg. Remarkably no one was killed. The Vitale gang surrendered, and police confiscated several sawed-off shotguns, revolvers, rifles and boxes of ammunition. Those arrested included Vitale, Salvatore Evola and Sam Catalanotte. One day later, Bloody John was charged with the murder of Pasquale D'Anna.

Three weeks later, one of the most audacious murders in Detroit gangland history took place. John Vitale was being held at the Wayne County Jail. On February 26, three Vitale partisans, including Salvatore Evola, Vito Renda and Joe Vitale, planned on visiting the boss. As the three men arrived at the facility, Deputy Philip Jasnowski noticed what appeared to be two Sicilian men loitering in the jail corridor. The deputy asked the men to state their business. "We are waiting for a friend," replied one of the men. At that moment, another deputy from across the hall opened the steel doors and told Jasnowski his dinner was ready. As he walked over to retrieve his dinner, Salvatore Evola, Vito Renda and Joe Vitale made their way into the corridor. As soon as the three men were visible, the two unidentified Sicilians pulled out revolvers and started shooting. "They seemed to be shooting all around and behind me," commented Jasnowksi. As bullets were flying, another deputy grabbed Evola and Vitale and pulled them away from the line of fire. Vito Renda, however, was hit twenty-one times. The gunmen escaped through the jail's front entrance. As the men ran for the escape vehicle, a squad car was pulling up front. Officer Albert Tansky jumped out and emptied his revolver at the fleeing men. He believed he hit at least one of the targets. The hit men jumped in the getaway car and headed north on Raynor Street. Police gave chase but lost the vehicle on Gratiot.

Evola, Vitale and Renda were transported to Detroit Receiving Hospital. Evola and Vitale suffered minor injuries, but Vito Renda was mortally wounded. As he was dying, Renda requested to speak with Judge Charles Wilkins. Although a potential conflict of interest, Wilkins was friendly with the Renda family. The judge arrived, and Renda identified Sam Giannola as one of the shooters.

Police immediately issued a warrant for Giannola's arrest. Two days later, Sam turned himself in. Naturally, the mafia boss hired Louis Colombo as his attorney. Giannola pleaded not guilty and claimed he was meeting with an insurance agent at the Chamber of Commerce building and could bear out the alibi. In the meantime, the gangland killings continued.

Salvatore Evola stands (back row, center), and Peter Corrado sits (bottom row, second from right). *Walter P. Reuther Library.*

On March 2, Antonio Frustace was gunned down while shopping at the Rosedale Court Grocery Store near Hamtramck. Two days later, Giannola bagman Alfio Beleti was shot and killed at the corner of Monroe Avenue and McDougall Street. Beleti was collecting money from fellow mobsters on behalf of Tony Giannola's widow.

The next day, the headlines featured another Giannola gangster on the rise. Five innocent bystanders were shot in a botched assassination attempt on Cesare "Chester" LaMare. As early as 1915, newspapers described LaMare as a local "gang leader" and "bully of the Sicilian colony." At the time, he was suspected of being behind a number of bombings and armed robberies. According to underworld legend, LaMare walked around with two bullets embedded in his body—battle scars from his time as a roughneck kid in Chicago. By 1919, LaMare was a trusted captain in the Giannola organization. He owned the Workingman's Café on Hastings. Chester was standing in front of the café, chatting with police, ironically enough, when a car pulled up and the men inside opened fire. LaMare was unharmed, but his boss was going to trial for the murder of Vito Renda.

Sam Giannola's trial began in early March. The proceedings started with much commotion. On the first day, Tony Renda and Paolo Mirabile were arrested for trying to enter court with pistols. Tony was Vito Renda's cousin, while Paolo was Pietro Mirabile's brother. Both men were released when they presented letters from Judge Wilkins permitting them to carry firearms.

In terms of the actual trial, reporters described Sam Giannola as unimpressed with the process. The mafia don frequently dozed off during proceedings. He had good reason to be relaxed. The prosecution's main witness was Officer Albert Tansky. But the officer could not say definitively if Sam Giannola was the man who shot Vito Renda. That was enough doubt for the jury, and the mob boss was acquitted.

The mobsters may have beaten the legal system, but law enforcement was still applying pressure. In late August, police raided a restaurant and hotel owned by Sam Giannola. Located on the corner of Brush and Congress, the establishment was popular with local public officials. Police, however, realized Giannola sold booze on the first floor and used the second floor as a brothel.

About a week later, police arrested members of the Vitale gang. A patrolman tried to stop a car and ask the men some questions when a passenger stuck a pistol out the window and aimed it at the officer's head. The car sped off, but when police caught up to it, they arrested six members

Santo Perrone testifying before Congress during the Kefauver hearings. Decades earlier, he was a top soldier in the Vitale gang. *Walter P. Reuther.*

of the Vitale gang. Among those detained included the ubiquitous Sal Evola and Alcamese gangsters Sam Catalanotte and Santo Perrone.

Detroit's Police Department was launching raids and rounding up gangsters, but it was not enough to stop the next major gangland assassination. On October 3, newspaper headlines read, "The King Is Dead."

REGIME CHANGE

According to underworld buzz, the warring factions agreed to a ceasefire during the fall of 1919. Details were unknown, but apparently Sam Giannola was satisfied enough to walk around Detroit unarmed and without bodyguards. One day the boss even strolled through rival Pietro Mirabile's turf near Russell Street and Monroe. On October 2, Giannola stopped at Mirabile's saloon and tried to cash a check. Underworld observers considered this odd. Mirabile technically served under Giannola's authority, but it was well known the two did not like each other. Apparently, the saloon owner would not accommodate the boss's request, so Giannola left the bar and walked over to Ferdinand Palma's bank. After cashing his check, the mafia king stepped outside and was riddled with twenty-eight bullets.

With Tony and Sam Giannola out of the way, Bloody John Vitale hoped to emerge as Detroit's undisputed mafia boss. Unfortunately for Vitale, the Giannola loyalists still represented a formidable group. Ignazio Caruso, the premier counterfeiter in Detroit's Italian underworld, led the group of loyalists. Plus, the faction included battle-tested gangsters like Vito Giannola and Chester LaMare. Most importantly, the group featured a number of deadly young Turks from Terrasini, including Joseph Zerilli, Vito Tocco and "Swinging" Sammie Serra.

Recognizing there was some unfinished business, the Vitale gang hit first. On January 12, 1920, Angelo Russo was shot to death. Santo Perrone admitted driving Russo to his execution but claimed he did not know who pulled the trigger. Perrone was arrested but later acquitted.

The flamboyant gangster Tony Alescio was next on the hit list. Alescio was twenty-eight years old and from Alcamo. He was known in the underworld as a thief and a gunman. He was arrested for being involved in the Peter Bosco murder but later released. Alescio was also a suspect in the Tony Giannola shooting. The young mobster was known for carrying wads of cash, wearing

Joe Zerilli as a young soldier in the Giannola Gang. *Scott M. Burnstein collection.*

expensive clothing and diamond rings and living in a chic apartment on Cass Avenue. On January 28, he was shot nine times in the chest.

In the meantime, investigators developed solid leads pertaining to Sam Giannola's murder. Calogero Arena was the lead suspect. Arena had ties to Detroit but at the time was living in Rochester, New York. The suspect fought extradition for several weeks before New York governor Al Smith signed the requisition papers. In early March, Arena finally faced trial in Detroit. One witness claimed they saw the suspect shoot Sam Giannola and run away with his revolver. The trial produced interesting information, but it was difficult to tell if Arena had taken a side in Detroit's mafia war, let alone shot Giannola. John Vitale, for example, admitted to knowing and having business relations with the accused. Vitale acted as Arena's surety during the trial. Giannola's widow, however, testified that Arena and her husband knew each other from working at the Wyandotte shipyards and the two were good friends. Furthermore, she stated the suspect had no motive for killing her husband. Other evidence suggested Arena was an underworld diplomat who acted as an intermediate between Giannola and his enemies. Between eyewitness testimony and evidence linking the suspect to both factions, the jury heard enough information to convict the New York gangster. Arena was sentenced to life in Jackson State Prison—only he never made it there. Judge Edward Jeffries granted the defense team's request for a retrial. On June 30, Arena was acquitted.

Arena left for New York a free man, yet back in Detroit, bodies continued to fall. Luigi Bono was shot to death in late July. The Giannola faction hit back hard in early August. Gunmen ambushed three members of the Vitale gang, killing Bloody John's nephews Tony Badalamenti and Giuseppe Manzella. Angelo Polizzi was also injured but survived the shooting. The three men were walking near the corner of Orleans and Catherine Streets when a car pulled up and opened fire.

The Giannola Gang aimed for the big prize next. John Vitale and his family lived on Russell Street. On August 17, John stood in front of his house waiting for his seventeen-year-old son, Joe, to pick him up. Joe Vitale was one of the men wounded in the Wayne County Jail shootout. The son appeared to be following in his father's footsteps. Joe was out on bail awaiting trial for shooting a police officer. As his son pulled up, the Vitales were unaware of the snipers camped out in a rented house across the street. Once John walked toward the vehicle, the snipers opened fire from the second-story window. Joe Vitale was hit and died instantly. John's wife ran out screaming and pulled her son's body out of the car. John ducked behind the car and avoided being hit.

Bloody John had little time to exact revenge. On September 28, John Vitale's lifeless body was found at three o'clock in the morning near the corner of Fourteenth Street and Marquette Avenue. Apparently, Vitale was on his way to meet someone at Michigan Central Station when he was murdered. Evidence suggested a setup. Vitale rarely traveled without his bodyguards. It is likely he trusted whoever set up the late-night meeting and felt secure traveling to the station.

Even without their leader, the Vitale faction had a few more shots to fire before capitulating. In mid-October, veteran gangster Andrea Licata was shot to death. Licata was one of the lead suspects in the murder of Detective Emmanuel Roggers. Less than ten minutes later, drive-by shooters hit up the grocery store of Ignazio Caruso. No one was hurt in the Caruso shooting.

THE PARTNERSHIP

With the Giannolas and Vitales dead, old wounds in the underworld finally started to heal. Evidence suggests that by 1921, the different mafia factions in Detroit were working together again. Ignazio Caruso was born in Trapani, Sicily, but in Detroit he was recognized as the official boss of the Italian

Detroit's mafia was on the verge of making millions trafficking illegal booze on the Detroit River. *Walter P. Reuther Library.*

underworld. Federal agents believed Caruso continued to run his large-scale counterfeiting operation. Secret Service agents also gathered interesting information during the surveillance operations of the Caruso grocery store. The feds noticed prominent members of the Giannola and Vitale factions interacting and engaging in business deals once again. Caruso had forged an alliance with Sam Catalanotte, who brought over the remnants of the Vitale gang. Investigators estimated there were fifty members in the Detroit mafia at the time.

Other evidence of the partnership surfaced in the fall of 1921 when police arrested two carloads of Mafiosi. Among those arrested were Joe Zerilli and Sammie Serra from Terrasini and Sal Evola and Sam Palazzolo from the old Vitale faction. Even veteran triggerman Giuseppe Cracchiolo was with the group. One year earlier, the two pairs of gangsters had been shooting at one another. Now they rode together. Police confiscated eleven guns, including revolvers and sawed-off shotguns. When asked what the gentlemen planned on doing with all these firearms, one suspect replied, "We were going hunting."

VICE, CORRUPTION AND THE RISE OF THE MAFIA

The young Turks and old-school gangsters put aside their differences in the interest of making money. This was a smart strategy because of the huge markets for booze, gambling and prostitution. And as the Roaring Twenties took off, Detroit was about to gather national attention for being the North American capital of vice and corruption.

CHAPTER 7

WICKED DETROIT

On July 13, 1926, the *New York Times* described Detroit as America's "most vile city." The paper formulated this opinion based on findings from the American Social Hygiene Association (ASHA). The group was a nongovernmental organization funded by the Rockefeller Foundation. Prominent Detroiters like Clara Ford (Henry's wife) and Judge Frank Murphy sat on the board. A number of influential civic organizations like the Detroit Citizens League, Wayne County Medical Society, League of Women Voters and YMCA were involved in the project. Overall, the ASHA examined the city's state of social morality.

Investigators with the ASHA wanted to measure levels of behavior associated with vice and conducted social survey research over a one-month period. The final conclusions were bleak. The report described "Detroit as the worst city in the United States in the matter of social evil." Researchers found 570 "disorderly houses" operating openly in a one-mile radius and 140 operating covertly. "Disorderly house" was a legal euphemism for brothel. In some cases, the site was openly used as a parlor house for prostitution, while in other examples, apartments and houses operated as brothels more discreetly. Investigators realized street prostitution was flourishing as well. Within the one-mile circle, which extended as far north as Warren Avenue, researchers documented over five hundred women working the streets. Evidence emerged of a human trafficking network smuggling women from foreign countries over to Canada and down through Detroit, Chicago and Cleveland. According to the final report, the sex trade was more widespread in Detroit than in larger cities like New York.

Adding to the city's social woes, the Narcotic Educational Association of Michigan claimed there were ten thousand "dope fiends" in Detroit. The association was talking about heroin addiction. Most of the heroin was smuggled through Windsor by the Italian mafia. According to the research, addicts were spending almost $36.5 million annually on drugs.

The ASHA report blamed Detroit's Police Department for most of the decadent behavior. Researchers accused the department of failing to enforce laws against vice. Mayor John W. Smith announced he was leading a concerted effort to reverse the trends. He applauded the ASHA for its efforts and asked the Rockefeller Foundation for support. Smith claimed the city would reorganize the police department and launch a new vice squad. The mayor did offer some sociological context and acknowledged that policing alone was not the answer. He talked about expanding economic opportunities and supporting social institutions to empower young people.

Although the city was wrestling with the problems of sex slavery and drug addiction, booze and gambling were still the cornerstones of the illicit economy. And more profits for gangsters meant more money to buy off politicians and law enforcement. Adding corruption and graft to a mix of vice and gangsterism produced a wicked decade.

The Rumrunner Capital of America

Entering the 1920s, Detroit was the epicenter of the automobile industry. Automobile-related companies included Ford, Dodge, Olds, Buick and Packard. By 1920, thirty-five thousand Detroiters were working in the automotive fields. A few years later, residents were driving 250,000 cars across city streets. Individuals from Europe and within North America flocked to Detroit to work in this promising sector. Between 1910 and 1930, the population tripled in size. Such developments prompted economic growth in other areas. Detroit's city streets, for example, were designed for horse carriages and electric streetcars. The consumer demand for automobiles corresponded to drastic changes in infrastructure. There was a need for construction workers and engineers as a result. The city started to look different, too, as the skyline expanded. When the Penobscot Building went up, it was the tallest structure in any city outside of New York or Chicago.

Police raid a blind pig and confiscate liquor. *Walter P. Reuther Library.*

With a growing population and automobiles to transport people, other industries popped up to satisfy consumer demand. The city saw an increase in a range of commercial enterprises from grocery stores and pharmacies to barbershops and clothing outlets. As with any burgeoning metropolis, some residents desired consumer goods from the alternative economy. Consequently, Detroit featured a thriving underground market. It was not difficult to find stolen goods, narcotics, sex and gambling in the city. Yet in the Roaring Twenties, alcohol was the supreme vice.

When Michigan first experimented with prohibition laws in 1916, Detroit counted 1,500 saloons and 800 illegal liquor joints within its boundaries. Seven years later, there were 10,000 blind pigs operating in the city. By the end of prohibition, 20,000 speakeasies and blind pigs were in operation. A significant number of these liquor enterprises were mom-and-pop operations. The *Literary Digest* reported, "There are blocks of the city in which every house is either a bootleg stand or a blind pig." Some independent producers cooked up a decent batch of back-alley

An aerial view of the Detroit River. Bootleggers in Detroit took advantage of the river's proximity to Canada. *Walter P. Reuther Library.*

beer, but often one would find a lesser quality of alcohol when buying from his neighbors. Consumers referred to such home-cooked products as "rot-gut." The problem with rot-gut was not just the taste—lower-quality spirits were sometimes toxic. To avoid low-end products, the consumer was better off buying imported alcohol.

Detroiters started off smuggling liquor from Ohio, but once Prohibition became national policy, residents looked across the river to Canada. The province of Ontario banned booze along with the United States. Nevertheless, there was a loophole in the policy. Local distillers could continue making alcohol for wet provinces like Quebec. As soon as the Volstead Act took effect in the United States, Detroiters and their Canadian neighbors set up networks to smuggle commercial-grade alcohol from Windsor to Detroit. The alcohol companies in Canada were no doubt complicit. By July 1920, liquor manufacturers had shipped 900,000 cases of booze to Windsor.

Once the product was in Windsor, sneaking booze across the river was relatively easy. The geological dimensions of the Detroit River made it almost impossible for law enforcement to police the waterways. Philip Mason writes, "The river was narrow, often less than a mile across, and could easily be crossed with a powerboat in less than five minutes. Numerous islands dotted the river providing hiding places for smugglers…All had excellent small harbors and inlets where smugglers could hide from the Coast Guard and police patrols." As Mason points out, Lake St. Clair, Lake Erie and the Detroit River were popular locations for thousands of "fishermen and pleasure boaters." Under such conditions, it was extraordinarily difficult for law enforcement to differentiate smugglers from leisurely civilians. The winter freezes did not stop smugglers either. Rumrunners would drive automobiles stocked with whiskey, beer and ale across the ice. Others pulled toboggans of whiskey across the frozen border.

The Windsor-Detroit nexus supplied 75 percent of America's alcohol during Prohibition. To give the reader a sense of scale, in 1925, rumrunners smuggled 666,000 gallons of liquor from Windsor. Three years later, smugglers were bringing over almost 2 million gallons. By 1930, the *Detroit Times* estimated bootleggers were bringing over 100,000 gallons a week. Once the liquor arrived in Detroit, bootleggers usually cut the product to enhance profits. In terms of retail, it was common to find alcohol sold in barbershops, butcher shops, pharmacies, grocery stores, candy stores and professional offices. Of course, Detroiters could also buy a drink at the plethora of speakeasies and blind pigs.

At the height of Prohibition, the illegal alcohol trade was one of the most profitable industries in Detroit, grossing $215 million a year. Overall, the illegal liquor trade was the city's second-largest employer after the automobile industry.

Detroiters were spending a lot of money on booze, while others made money on the liquor trade. Even if they were caught by law enforcement, most pleaded guilty and paid a fine. At the local level, the Recorder's Court was so overwhelmed with Prohibition cases that it would dismiss hundreds of charges a year.

Yet the liquor business could be a violent endeavor. Between 1919 and 1923, law enforcement attributed ninety-seven homicides to the liquor trade. Some of the killings were linked to organized crime. Mafia bootleggers would kill independent rivals and non-connected rumrunners without a second thought. Meanwhile, equally violent non-Italian syndicates like the Purple Gang, the Little Jewish Navy, the Tallman Gang and the Legs Laman Gang terrorized the competition with hijackings, kidnappings, extortion and murders. Law enforcement developed a lethal reputation during the period

Police raid an illegal still and dump the booze. *Walter P. Reuther Library.*

as well. Between 1927 and 1928, Detroit Police shot to death 70 persons and wounded 134. By 1929, federal agents had killed 44 individuals over Prohibition-related confrontations in Detroit.

Despite the risk of violence, most bootleggers stayed in the racket and in the process accumulated political influence. The so-called saloon-control of local politics preexisted the ban on booze. In fact, groups like the Anti-Saloon League, the Michigan Dry Federation and the Detroit Citizens League argued that Prohibition would reduce local political corruption. During the early 1900s, political observers lamented the political influence of beer barons and saloon keepers. According to critics, the saloon owners and brewers controlled Detroit's City Council and the local Board of Education.

Billy Boushaw stood out as one of the most colorful and politically powerful tavern owners. He owned the infamous Bucket of Blood flophouse on Atwater Street. The establishment had a reputation for attracting hustlers, thieves and gamblers. As a precinct boss, Boushaw was considered a political kingmaker in the area. It was difficult to to win local office without his blessing. Boushaw and other men from the liquor industry formed an interest group known as the Royal Ark. The Ark handpicked members of the local school board. Such an arrangement gave bosses like Boushaw influence over who the board hired. The bosses would hand out teaching, administrative and janitorial jobs to those who supported the Ark. Supporting Boushaw meant access to building and construction contracts, too. Such political manipulation permeated the city government. William P. Lovett described the city treasury as a "Christmas grab-bag." To counter the graft machine, influential Detroiters like Henry Ford, J.L. Hudson and John C. Lodge bankrolled dry political groups.

Yet even after the nation adopted Prohibition, the booze industry continued to wield influence over local politics. The *Literary Digest* claimed "no candidate for mayor, judge, congress, or governor or any other office had any chance" to win election without the Royal Ark's endorsement. Furthermore, Prohibition was never popular in urban areas like Detroit. To illustrate their populist credentials, political candidates in Detroit often visited pool halls and blind pigs. Politicians also solicited support from gambling dens. If drinking was an accepted activity, then gambling was the second most popular vice in wicked Detroit.

Big Shots

After booze, gambling was the next biggest organized crime industry in Detroit. The policy racket was one of the most popular forms of gambling in the city. "Policy" referred to a type of lottery game. Gamblers bet that a particular sequence of numbers would be pulled out of the lottery drum. Policy was popular in low-income neighborhoods because one could place small bets. By the late 1920s, there were over thirty policy houses operating in Detroit. The number of policy houses actually declined over the decade, but not due to lack of interest. When organized criminals realized how much they could make through illegal lotteries, the gangsters started taking over. They put the independent operators out of business and consolidated the number of houses. The racket was attractive to gangsters because it did not require a lot of capital to set up a game. Once you had a cylinder, a table, some rubber tubing containing the numbers and a person to grind out the sequences, you

Typical gambling house in Detroit. *Walter P. Reuther Library.*

were in business. Runners circulated throughout the neighborhood, going door-to-door in some cases, soliciting bets. Naturally, pool halls and blind pigs were popular locations to find customers. And, of course, the odds favored the house. Some illegal lotteries advertised three-hundred-to-one odds, while others claimed you had a five-hundred-to-one chance. More sober observers, however, argued the real odds were about six thousand to one. Generally, the house was taking in around 80 percent. An unidentified policy big shot told the *Detroit News* he was taking in $6,000 a day, and the house employed over 150 men as runners, security guards and loan-sharks. The newspaper estimated Detroiters were betting between $50,000 and $60,000 a day on numbers.

Slot machines were popular as well. Thousands of machines existed throughout the city. It was not uncommon to find a one-armed bandit in local restaurants and other small businesses. To find some real action, though, Detroiters went to a gambling den. There you had access to slot machines, poker, blackjack, roulette and dice games. Gambling joints were so profitable that the house would often provide free transportation. They might arrange to pick you up from a particular blind pig or pool hall. Not as lucrative as liquor, the average gambling den was still taking in $1 million a year.

Prior to the election of Mayor John W. Smith, the gambling houses operated with impunity. High-profile gambling big shots in the city included Lefty Clark, Dan Sullivan, Denny Murphy, Doc Brady and the Wertheimer brothers. Prominent public officials were known to associate with such men and frequent their establishments.

Muckraking reporter Walter W. Liggett visited one of the gambling dens and provided a colorful description:

> *Entrance is obtained through several winding passageways and a visitor must go through two rooms filled with hard boiled "gorillas." Upstairs, before the iron barred door is opened, would be entrants—women as well as men—are thoroughly frisked by several agile gunmen who confiscate all weapons. At least twenty more gunmen are on guard inside and in addition there is an armed "look-out" over each one of the twenty tables. Two machine gun nests have built high into the walls and vigilant gunners can command any portion of the floor space with their death-dealing muzzles masked behind shutters.*

Some politicians spoke out against the industry. City Councilman Fred W. Castator claimed it cost the taxpayers $300,000 a year in social assistance to support the families of degenerate gamblers. In 1923, the Smith administration launched an anti-gambling campaign. He ordered the police to start raiding the most notorious gambling dens. Sledgehammer squads would burst into the location, destroy the gambling paraphernalia and padlock the place. The police arrested hundreds of gangsters associated with gambling and arrested thousands of Detroiters for frequenting such establishments. Smith convinced the gambling bosses he was serious, and the big shots relocated their operations to the suburbs of Wayne County. They set up gambling dens in cities like Ecorse and Grosse Pointe. Subsequently, Wayne County sheriffs raided one of Lefty Clark's gambling joints in Ecorse. Having been pushed out of Detroit, Clark decided to fight back. Not long after the raid, Sheriff Ira Wilson's barn burned down, and thirty of his cattle were slaughtered. Wilson backed down and refused to assist Michigan State Police in their anti-gambling raids.

Detroit's original gangsters found more hospitable locations in smaller cities throughout Wayne County, and no city was more mobbed up than Hamtramck. Located within the geographical boundaries of Detroit,

Police raid a gambling den on Michigan Avenue. *Walter P. Reuther Library.*

Hamtramck featured more blind pigs per capita than most big cities. The Dodge Main factory provided the city's economic engine. Dodge Main produced 140,000 cars a year and employed approximately twenty thousand workers. After a grueling day at the plant, many workers enjoyed the assortment of vices available within walking distance.

The old Giannola gang member Chester LaMare was the vice lord of Hamtramck. He owned a handful of saloons, gambling parlors and brothels. Known on the streets as "Big Chet," the crime boss would hold court at the Venice Café. All the other blind pigs in the city had to pay LaMare a mob tax. The mob tax was an act of extortion. Independent racketeers had to pay a tax to LaMare for the privilege of operating on his territory or suffer the consequences. The mob boss also had the mayor on his payroll.

Mayor Peter Jezweski was one of the most notorious public officials in the Detroit area. Jezweski ordered the Hamtramck police to ignore the gambling joints and saloons in the city. Officers were especially warned to stay away from establishments run by LaMare. The Wayne County prosecutor asked the Michigan State Police to launch an investigation. According to the state police's final report, the mayor interfered with investigations and "demoralized" the police force. Former police chief Mark Berlinger offered

Police raid a gambling den. Slot machines were popular in Detroit. *Walter P. Reuther Library.*

stunning information to state investigators. He claimed the mayor was furious with him after he ordered a raid on one of LaMare's gambling dens. Jezweski hollered at the police chief, "What in the hell is the matter with you?" During the raid, Berlinger confiscated $500 worth of silver pieces, yet the mayor ordered him to return it to the mob boss immediately. One night, an officer stopped by the Venice Café to investigate, and LaMare's henchmen beat the man with two-by-fours. Jezweski told Berlinger to let it go.

During the day, the Venice Café was a popular location for public officials to wine and dine. However, the restaurant stayed open till six o'clock in the morning. According to the Michigan State Police report, patrons would stay up all night drinking, playing cards and enjoying the company of "loose women." LaMare and his crew used the café as their headquarters. Berlinger explained how Big Chet led a crew of about fifteen men, including the infamous mafia enforcer "Black" Leo Cellura. The former police chief noted that none of the men held legitimate employment.

Eventually, Governor Alex Groesbeck ordered the Michigan State Police to intervene. Over a fifteen-month period, state police raided almost three hundred vice parlors. LaMare was arrested for violating Prohibition laws but received a minor sentence. The slap on the wrist included a modest fine and probation. Even Mayor Jezweski was indicted. The mayor had ordered his own police force to transport truckloads full of liquor. Jezweski was found guilty and served his sentence at Leavenworth Prison. Local politicians were not the only ones on the take. Soon, federal law enforcement officers were in the corruption hot seat.

THE GRAFT TRUST

To fight the illegal booze trade, Uncle Sam devoted significant resources to the Detroit area. In addition to thirty speedboats, the U.S. Coast Guard maintained two seventy-five-foot cutters and one thirty-six-foot patrol boat. Federal law enforcement personnel included 150 U.S. Customs inspectors, thirty Coast Guardsmen, thirty Treasury officials and ten Narcotics Squad agents. Yet investigators claimed 50 to 75 percent of the illegal liquor trafficked across the Detroit River made it to shore unimpeded. The geographic characteristics of the river explained some of the bootleggers' success—but not all of it.

In 1928, the feds conducted an eight-month corruption investigation in Detroit. Customs collector Carey D. Feguson and U.S. district attorney John R. Watkins ordered the investigation. The grand jury concluded federal inspectors had collected more than $500,000 in bribes. By December, fourteen U.S. Customs inspectors had been indicted by the grand jury on bribery charges. Watkins noted, however, that one hundred additional federal agents were implicated in the graft scheme. Officials from the Coast Guard and Bureau of Immigration were linked to the corruption scandal. Newspapers labeled the gang of dirty officials the "Graft Trust."

The scheme worked a few different ways. Each night, a payoff man from the bootlegger gang would meet with crooked agents. Corrupted officials could make anywhere from $100 to $1,000 a month depending on shipment volume. Generally, dirty cops charged $0.25 for each case of beer and $1.00 per case of whiskey. Bootleggers and the graft trust worked out so-called free nights too. Under this scenario, smugglers paid by the hour rather than by the case. The bootlegger would pay for a four- or five-hour slot of time. Crooked officials would guarantee no inspections during the paid hours. As part of the deal, the bootleggers would tip off federal officials regarding shipments by the competition. In other words, bootleggers would provide

LOOKOUT ON AMERICAN SIDE

RUNNER WITH GLASSES AWAITING SIGNAL

LOADED OUTBOARD SPEED BOAT

Bootleggers wait for the signal to cross the river and score booze. *Walter P. Reuther Library.*

information about smugglers not affiliated with the graft trust. That gave customs agents an opportunity to bust up some shipments and give the appearance they were doing their job.

Several bootleggers were implicated in the corruption scandal, yet investigators singled out Peter Licavoli as the Italian underworld's top payoff man. Licavoli captained the River Gang, a crew of Mafiosi running rackets in the downriver area. In addition to bootlegging, the River Gang was involved in gambling, extortion, auto theft, kidnapping and armed robbery. Peter's brother, Thomas "Yonnie" Licavoli, was a prominent member of the crew. Although the brothers were born in St. Louis, Missouri, the Licavoli family traced its heritage to Terrasini, Sicily. The brothers got their start working with the legendary Egan's Rats gang in St. Louis. Recognizing the lucrative potential of illegal liquor, the brothers relocated to Detroit. Soon, their cousins "Horseface" Pete Licavoli and James "Jack White" Licavoli left St. Louis and joined the River Gang. Relocating also made sense because of Detroit's large Terrasinese community. In the Motor City, the Licavolis linked up with other Terrasini gangsters, including "Scarface" Joe Bommarito, Joseph "Joe Misery" Moceri and "Machinegun" Pete Corrado. Notorious bank robber Frank Cammarata married Peter Licavoli's sister and was an

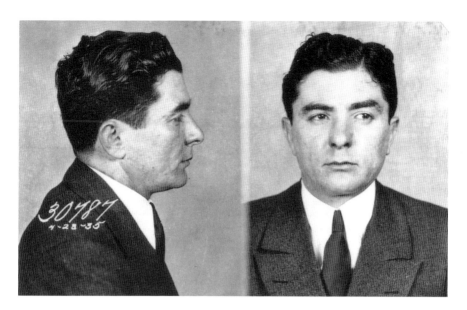

River Gang boss Peter Licavoli. *Scott M. Burnstein collection.*

important member of the River Gang. Mafiosi from Cinisi like Dominic Badalamenti and Salvatore Palazzolo also worked with the gang.

Eventually, information leaked that Peter Licavoli was bribing customs officials. A federal grand jury indicted the River Gang leader on November 4, 1929. Border Patrol agents tracked Licavoli down and pulled his car over on the Belle Isle Bridge. While being questioned, the mob boss pushed away from the agents, jumped in his car and sped off. Police fired twenty shots, but somehow Licavoli escaped. Fearing police had shoot-to-kill orders, the River Gang boss turned himself in. Peter Licavoli was found guilty and sent to Leavenworth Prison for two years.

Allegations of corruption did not end with the Graft Trust scandal. By 1930, Charles Bowles was mayor of Detroit, and standards for integrity in government were at an all-time low. The folly of the Bowles administration set in motion one of the most shocking public murders in Detroit's underworld history. Gangsters had been killing other gangsters, but they were about to target a civilian. And not just any civilian—the mob was taking aim at a beloved media celebrity.

CHAPTER 8

KILLING BUCKLEY

William Cannon and George Collins did not belong to a specific gang. Instead, the men operated independently, getting involved in scams and rackets as opportunities presented themselves. Cannon had served time at Jackson State Prison on armed robbery charges, while Collins was a suspected extortionist. Eventually, the two linked up and set off for Chicago, hoping to get involved in the bootlegging business. The two hoods would also impersonate police officers and extort other criminals. Chicago Police became aware of the pair and described them as "lower tier gangsters." By the summer of 1930, Cannon and Collins were back in Detroit setting up narcotics deals. Once in the Motor City, they connected with Michael Stizel, a former associate of gambling big shot Lefty Clark.

On July 3, the three men stopped at a pool hall on Woodward and Charlotte Avenue. After playing a few games, the gangsters had enough and walked toward Cannon's car, parked in front of the LaSalle Hotel on Adelaide Street. Collins and Stizel noticed two surly looking men standing in front of the hotel lobby entrance. "They're certainly tough-looking mugs," observed Collins. Stizel and his gangland partners entered Cannon's car, and as they pulled away, at least two "tough-looking" men walked toward the vehicle, pulled out their weapons and opened fire. After shooting Cannon and Collins to death, the two hit men calmly walked through the LaSalle Hotel lobby and left through the Woodward exit. Stizel was injured but survived the shooting.

The shooting was brazen even by Detroit gangland standards. The murders took place around 6:30 p.m. on a Thursday. Dozens of hotel guests

Popular broadcaster and political reformer Gerald Buckley. *Walter P. Reuther Library.*

were coming and going through the lobby, and numerous civilians were in front of the hotel when the gunmen opened fire.

Interestingly, a popular local radio personality nearly witnessed the killings. The WMBC studios were located inside the LaSalle Hotel. Gerald Buckley was broadcasting his show when he heard gunshots. The timing seemed apropos. Buckley had been using his show as a forum to criticize corruption and gangland violence in the city. Unfortunately for him, the hotel lobby shootings offered a preview of his own fate.

CRIMEBUSTER OR CRIME BOSS?

Gerald Buckley was broadcasting during precarious times. The stock market crashed on October 24, 1929, triggering the Great Depression. Like most of the country, Detroit was experiencing economic turmoil. Detroit started off with a diverse industrial economy, but by 1929, the city was basically a one-industry town. If the automotive sector faltered, so did Detroit. The Great

EARLY ORGANIZED CRIME IN DETROIT

Depression rolled through Detroit evaporating half of the city's automotive jobs. Detroit's largest bank was declared insolvent, and its main competitor was on life support. More than 150,000 Detroiters lived without financial support as the unemployment rate hit 40 percent. Predictably, home foreclosures were on the rise and shantytowns appeared throughout the city.

Under such economic conditions, Buckley's populist message resonated with a wide audience. Buckley championed a nationalized pension system and jobs programs for the unemployed. He also clamored for honesty in government. Considering the dire economic circumstances the average person faced, Buckley was offended when public officials engaged in bribery, graft and embezzlement. The popular radio host held particular scorn for Detroit's mayor: Charles Bowles.

Buckley accused Bowles of looking the other way while gangsters pillaged the city. The implication was the mayor was on the take. Charles Bowles ascended to the position after defeating John W. Smith in Detroit's 1929 mayoral election. Controversy surrounded the Bowles administration from the very beginning. Within days of taking office, the mayor's office faced its first public corruption crisis.

On January 2, 1930, an assassination attempt was made on police inspector Henry Garvin. Garvin had a distinguished arrest record, putting away some of the city's most notorious stickup men. He was a well-known adversary of the Purple Gang and Legs Laman gang and headed up the department's bomb squad. The inspector was driving to work when he noticed a black sedan tailing him. The car pulled up to the right side of Garvin's car and crowded the vehicle, making it difficult for him to maneuver away. Once they had the inspector in their sights, the occupants of the sedan aimed their shotguns out of the window and blasted away. Garvin was hit in the head and the left arm. Tragically, an innocent bystander was shot. Eleven-year-old Lois Bartlett was on her way to school when she was hit by a stray shotgun slug. Garvin was at the hospital when he heard the news about Bartlett and insisted his personal physician attend to the girl. Both victims survived the shooting.

Detroiters were understandably outraged by the attack. Gangland violence was alarming enough, but now a prominent police inspector and an innocent schoolgirl were caught in the crossfire. Charles Bowles had barely taken over as mayor, yet citizens demanded something be done. Bowles had little to say about the shootings, but the Detroit Police Department suspected one gang was responsible.

Investigators believed the River Gang was behind the hit. Licavoli's crew had a violent reputation. Police suspected the gang was responsible for dozens

Members of the infamous River Gang. Joe "Misery" Moceri stands second to left. His brother Leo stands to his right. *Scott M. Burnstein collection.*

of underworld slayings in the Great Lakes area. Licavoli's triggermen were likely responsible for the 1928 murder of rival gang leader Joe Tallman.

On January 3, police arrested Joe "Misery" Moceri on attempted murder charges. Moceri was Peter Licavoli's right-hand man. His brothers Leo "Lips" and James Moceri were arrested, too. An incident from six months earlier had led police to believe the Moceri brothers had it in for Garvin. The bomb squad inspector had been investigating the River Gang for a string of burglaries and hijackings. During one encounter, Garvin was arresting a member of the gang when Joe Moceri interfered. Garvin and Moceri fought, and it ended when the inspector busted Moceri's nose. Witnesses heard Joe "Misery" promise to "get even."

After locking up the Moceri brothers, police arrested the River Gang leader the next day. Ironically, Peter Licavoli had just turned himself in regarding charges that he had bribed U.S. Customs officials. He was released on $10,000 bail, yet Detroit Police arrested him on attempted murder before he could walk out the door. Detectives rounded up other prominent members of the gang, including Dominic Badalamenti and Mike Rubino.

The investigation took a surprising turn one month later. Detective Adolph Van Coppenolle met with the Police Trial Board on February 6. He faced charges regarding "conduct unbecoming an officer." During the hearing, the detective alleged Henry Garvin's shooting was the result of a bad deal between the inspector and the Legs Laman gang. Van Coppenolle claimed he met with underworld informants at the Book-Cadillac Hotel in late October 1929. According to Van Coppenolle, the informants warned him Garvin was going to be hit because he had double-crossed members of the Laman gang. Van Coppenolle told the board the Laman mob paid Garvin $20,000 to have Legs Laman tried on extortion rather than kidnapping charges. Apparently, Garvin accepted the cash but did not fix the charges.

Other officers appeared before the board accusing Garvin of being dirty. Police sergeant Max Waldfogel of the Black Hand Squad described Garvin as the head of a kidnapping ring. According to the sergeant, Garvin would identify kidnapping targets, give gangs the information and then collect a percentage of the ransom. Waldfogel claimed kidnappings were on the rise in Detroit because Garvin was supervising the snatch rackets.

Underworld figures testified before the board, too. Purple Gang associate Morris "Big Chief" Rappaport alleged that Garvin tried to shake him down. Rappaport was winning big at Johnny Ryan's gambling joint in Grosse Pointe when he ran into Garvin. The Big Chief said the inspector was shooting dice. According to Rappaport, Garvin knew the Big Chief won big and arrested him later that evening. The Purple gangster claimed Garvin offered to let him go for a $4,000 bribe.

Such stunning allegations generated a media circus. There were some discrepancies, however, with Van Coppenolle's accusations. He would assign different dates to specific events each time he testified. The detective also provided information that conflicted with his earlier statements. Meanwhile, reporters went to Jackson State Prison to interview Legs Laman. The gangster dismissed allegations that his gang tried to pay off or assassinate Garvin. "I have no friends. I belong to no gang. If my friends wanted to help me, I think they would contribute to the support of my wife and child rather than plot to shoot up some police officer," added Laman. The media frenzy eventually passed, and Garvin was reinstated but no longer as head of the bomb squad.

OPEN CITY

The Bowles administration survived the Garvin scandal, yet more corruption allegations emerged. On March 11, Bowles announced a major shakeup of the police department. To begin, several experienced officers were forced into retirement. The mayor also centralized the vice squad. Prior to the centralization plan, individual precinct commanders oversaw the enforcement of vice laws. A number of veteran policemen, including Bowles's own police chief, publicly disagreed with the reorganization plan.

Considering the Garvin scandal, it seemed that a shakeup of the department was in order. Reporters, however, noted that flagrant violations of liquor and gambling laws became the norm after the March reorganization plan. Furthermore, the numbers of burglaries and robberies nearly doubled once Bowles took office. Critics accused the mayor of accepting campaign donations from criminals and promising lax police enforcement in return.

The mayor was no stranger to controversy. He had the notorious distinction of being the Ku Klux Klan's favorite politician. And while Detroit had the highest unemployment rate of any big American city, Bowles favored cuts to social assistance programs. The public nearly rioted when the mayor raised streetcar fees. Critics also took issue with his political appointees. Bowles picked his personal friend to head up the Department of Street Railways. He also appointed one of his campaign workers to head up the Civil Service Commission. Both department heads were unapologetic about cronyism in the administration. Former police chief and millionaire investor John Gillespie was Bowles's most controversial appointment. Gillespie was the mayor's public works commissioner. In that capacity, Gillespie handed out sweetheart deals to personal friends and political supporters of the mayor.

Notorious Detroit mayor Charles Bowles. *Walter P. Reuther Library.*

113

By early May, enough Detroiters were fed up with Bowles to organize a recall effort. The Kentucky Derby indirectly sparked Detroit's political resistance. While Bowles and Gillespie were attending the annual horse racing event, police chief Harold Emmons ordered more robust policing efforts. Several gambling joints, brothels and blind pigs were raided during the mayor's absence. The media applauded Emmons, but Bowles was furious when he returned. Bowles demanded Emmons's resignation, and when the police chief refused, the mayor fired him. One day later, the Citizens' Committee for the Recall of Mayor Bowles was formed.

The *Detroit News* and the *Detroit Free Press* endorsed the recall, and political groups like the Citizens League led the effort. The campaign turned ugly right away. Bowles accused the newspapers of leading a political witch hunt. Conspiracy theorists and bigoted supporters of Bowles also joined the fray. Ku Klux Klan leaders blamed Catholics for starting the recall effort, while Henry Ford claimed Jews had taken over the Citizens League. Fighting the recall, Bowles led one of Detroit's first modern media campaigns, spending

"Scarface" Joe Bommarito is suspect number one on the far left. The lineup also includes James Licavoli and James Moceri. *Walter P. Reuther Library Collection.*

lavishly on radio advertisements. John Gillespie served as campaign manager and bought a fleet of automobiles to transport voters to the polls. Overall, the mayor's team spent $100,000 on the campaign.

The vote took place on July 22. It didn't help Bowles that newspapers labeled the month "Bloody July." Beginning on July 3, the city witnessed ten gangland slayings, including the murders of Cannon and Collins. When asked what he thought about all the murders, Bowles responded that as long as gangsters killed one another, they performed a public service. Such callous comments did go over well with voters. On Tuesday, July 22, voters finally had their say. And many Detroiters tuned in to Gerald Buckley's show to hear the results.

THE VOICE OF THE PEOPLE IS SILENCED

Gerald Buckley was born into an old Detroit family and grew up in the Irish district of Detroit known as Corktown. He completed his law degree at the Detroit College of Law and after graduation joined Ford Motor Company as a private investigator. Henry Ford asked Buckley to investigate U.S. senator Truman H. Newberry. Newberry defeated Ford in Michigan's 1918 U.S. Senate race. The campaign was filled with mudslinging as Newberry accused Henry of helping his son Edsel dodge the draft. After the election, Ford alleged Newberry used illegal funds to win the race. Newberry and several of his staffers were eventually convicted for violating campaign finance laws. Newberry ended up resigning from office.

The case inspired Buckley to champion the cause of good government. He left Ford Motor Company and joined WMBC to start a radio career in 1928. During his nightly broadcasts, Buckley mixed his populist economic message with a ferocious critique of vice in the city. Going after vice and corruption did not endear him to the underworld. The radio crusader would frequently out public officials for associating with gangsters. He also demanded law enforcement crack down on gambling and prostitution. As a result, it was common for Buckley to receive death threats at the station.

Buckley was particularly offended by the Bowles administration. For the radio host, Bowles embodied everything that was wrong with Detroit politics. Subsequently, he devoted more and more broadcast time to criticizing the mayor's tolerance of vice and outlawry. At one point, unidentified parties offered Buckley $25,000 to lay off Bowles, but the radio host refused.

On July 22, Buckley had the satisfaction of reporting the recall election results. The recall campaign was successful, with 120,863 voting for and 89,907 voting against. Prior to the election, no large American city had successfully recalled a mayor before. Unfortunately for Buckley, he did not have long to celebrate.

After signing off the air, Buckley decided to hang out at the LaSalle. Hotel employees witnessed the radio host accept a phone call around 12:15 a.m. They overhead him repeat "yes" several times, followed by the phrase "in about an hour."

The Buckley murder scene at the LaSalle Hotel. *Walter P. Reuther Library.*

At 1:45 a.m., Buckley was sitting in the hotel lobby reading the paper when gunmen walked up to him and fired several rounds. It was a massacre. Buckley was hit eleven times, including six bullets in the back of the head. The murder occurred less than fifty yards from the locations of the shootings of Cannon and Collins.

When word of the assassination hit the news cycle, it was a bigger story than the recall. Governor Fred Green was outraged and announced he would send the National Guard in to restore order in Detroit. Mayor Bowles and his new police chief Thomas Wilcox refused the governor's assistance. Green recommended that Bowles and Wilcox at least let Michigan State Police lead the investigation, but again the governor was turned down.

Immediately, supporters of Buckley accused the underworld and Bowles of conspiring to kill the popular broadcaster. Former Wayne County prosecutor Paul Buckley claimed his brother was killed because of the recall campaign.

The investigation continued, but in the meantime Buckley's funeral was another spectacle. Close to fifty thousand mourners arrived at Mt. Olivet Cemetery to honor the slain radio personality. Detroit Recorder's Court judge Frank Murphy read the eulogy. He referred to Buckley as a "man of the people, by the people and for the people."

Buckley's fans were still mourning when police arrested their first suspect.

The night of the murder, investigators noticed hotel resident and River Gang associate Angelo Livecchi acting suspicious. Gus Reno was at his taxicab stand and saw Livecchi leaving the hotel lobby moments after the shooting. Hotel security also saw Livecchi leaving the scene of the crime. After arresting the suspect, police announced they were looking for three more River Gang members: Thomas "Yonnie" Licavoli, Ted Pizzino and Frank Cammarata. Ultimately, the Wayne County Circuit Court authorized a twenty-three-man grand jury to investigate the murder.

The investigation turned political, however, once Buckley's opponents emerged with allegations of their own. The *Detroit Times* was the one paper in town friendly to the Bowles administration. The *Times* published stories about Buckley's reputation as a womanizer and suggested the radio host was involved in blackmail. Reporters also published a story that linked the broadcaster to the Legs Laman gang. Even more provocative, Thomas Wilcox announced he had a signed affidavit from a known bootlegger named Frank Chock alleging Buckley was an extortionist. Overall, Buckley's political opponents accused him of being a hypocritical shakedown artist who got what was coming to him.

Buckley murder suspect Ted Pizzino and his family. *Walter P. Reuther Library.*

Buckley's defenders responded promptly. Wayne County prosecutor James Chenot described the Legs Laman rumors as "absolutely false." Next, Buckley family attorneys produced a second affidavit in which Frank Chock repudiated his earlier testimony. Chock claimed he did not know how to read or write English and was hoodwinked into signing the first affidavit. In the meantime, Buckley fans flooded the *Detroit Times* with angry letters accusing the paper of running a smear campaign.

While the public debated Buckley's character, investigators hauled in another suspect. Ted Pizzino was criminal partners with Livecchi and co-owned the Kit Kat Club with "Black" Leo Cellura. Pizzino was hiding out in New York when detectives received a tip. An informant told police the suspect was preparing to flee to Italy. In one of Detroit's first criminal investigations to utilize modern aircraft, detectives rushed to Ford Airport and boarded a flight to New York. Pizzino unsuccessfully fought extradition and was back in Detroit to face charges.

The Buckley grand jury met throughout the fall and in late January 1931 announced more indictments. Livecchi and Pizzino were already under indictment, but the grand jury added five more suspects, including Peter Licavoli and "Scarface" Joe Bommarito.

The prosecution eventually dropped charges against Licavoli, but the other defendants faced trial in March. Linking the gangsters to the corrupt Bowles administration was crucial to the prosecution. One of Mayor Bowles's former ward captains took the stand and connected the mobsters to Norman B. Smith. Smith was a big contributor to the Bowles campaign and a known bootlegger. The witness claimed he and Smith met with Angelo Livecchi, Ted Pizzino, "Black" Leo Cellura and mob heavyweight Angelo Meli. According to the testimony, Cellura boasted of

Angelo Meli was a high-ranking member of the Detroit mafia. *Walter P. Reuther Library.*

Angelo Livecchi was tried for the murder of Gerald Buckley. *Walter P. Reuther Library.*

donating $11,000 to the Bowles campaign. When the broadcaster's name came up, Livecchi said someone should "cut Buckley's tongue out."

Defense attorneys countered with legal maneuvers of their own. The defense team was able to suppress certain evidence. Fearing reprisal, a crucial eyewitness refused to testify. The person was held in contempt, but that did not help the prosecution. After deliberating for more than thirty hours, the jury reached its verdict: "not guilty."

Buckley probably would have suspected such an outcome. His murder and subsequent investigation did, however, finish Bowles's political career. Bowles lost the runoff election to Frank Murphy. The former judge fired Wilcox and replaced him with criminologist James Watkins. Murphy and Watkins reorganized the police force, placing more emphasis on scientific policing methods and utilizing technology. They also implemented anti-corruption reforms and launched an aggressive anti-gambling campaign.

Murphy's reformed police department was about to face a serious test. Detroit was on the verge of another full-scale mafia war.

CHAPTER 9

NEW ORDER

On the streets of New York City, he was known as "Joe the Boss," but Giuseppe Masseria was born in Marsala, Sicily. In New York, Masseria headed up one of the largest Italian crime organizations on the East Coast.

On April 15, 1931, Joe the Boss traveled to Coney Island to have lunch with his young lieutenant Charlie "Lucky" Luciano. The pair met at the Nuovo Villa Tammaro restaurant. Masseria's bodyguards were also present. Joe the Boss did not travel without security. His car was fitted with steel armor and bullet-proof windows. The boss had to be extra cautious considering the New York underworld was in the midst of an all-out mafia war. Masseria's organization was battling New York's Castellammarese mafia led by Salvatore Maranzano.

Back in Sicily, Maranzano was an important leader in the Magaddino-Bonventre alliance and sworn enemy of the Buccellatos. He arrived in America in 1925 and within a few years replaced Nicolo Schiro as head of the Castellammarese mafia in New York.

No doubt Joe the Boss felt comfortable sitting with bodyguards and his gangster understudy Luciano. After consuming copious amounts of pasta, clams and lobster, Masseria and his men decided to play cards. At approximately 3:00 p.m., Luciano excused himself from the table to use the restroom. Once Lucky was out of sight, a hit-squad burst into the restaurant and lit up Joe the Boss. He was hit five times and died instantly.

By the time police arrived, Luciano had the perfect alibi: he was in the john and did not see anything. The execution was a setup, of course. Luciano

```
                RESTRICTED-FOR OFFICIAL USE ONLY
                                                 INTERNATIONAL LIST
NAME            : Charles LUCIANO
                                                 NO. 198
ALIASES         : Charlie Lucania; Lucky Luciano;
                  Charles Lane; Charles Reid; Charles
                  Ross.

DESCRIPTION     : Born in Italy; age 48 years; hgt.
                  5'10"; wgt. 140 lbs.

LOCALITIES        Was deported from U.S.A. to Italy
FREQUENTED      : on February 11, 1946; in 1946 re-
                  sided in Naples; repeated informa-
                  tion indicates he will return to
                  Cuba or Mexico and possible to the
                  United States.

CRIMINAL          Frank Costello; Meyer Lansky; Ben-
ASSOCIATES      : jamin Siegel; Frank Milano of Akron
                  Ohio; Nicola Gentile.

FACSIMILE OF
SIGNATURE                                        See Reverse
```

Federal Bureau of Narcotics file on Charles "Lucky" Luciano. *National Archives.*

negotiated a deal behind Masseria's back. The deal was simple: kill Joe the Boss and take over his organization. There was one catch, though. Lucky would take over Masseria's operations, but Maranzano would be *capo di tutti capi* (the boss of all bosses).

Luciano would not stand for this and took out Maranzano, too. Luciano dissolved any notion of one supreme mafia boss and instead encouraged his colleagues to settle disputes diplomatically. Following Luciano's lead, the American mafia emerged stronger and better organized than ever. As a result, Italian American crime families radically altered the underworld landscape not only in North America but also globally. The Castellammarese War set these developments in motion, and the first shots were fired in Detroit.

FRACTURE

The Roaring Twenties were prosperous years for Detroit's organized crime groups. It was also a relatively peaceful decade for the Italian mafia, at least internally. For the first time in its history, Detroit's mafia was operating as a cohesive unit. This was in large part due to the leadership of Salvatore "Singing Sam" Catalanotte. Singing Sam brokered the peace between the

VICE, CORRUPTION AND THE RISE OF THE MAFIA

RESTRICTED-FOR OFFICIAL USE ONLY   NATIONAL LIST

NAME : Joseph CATALANOTTE   NO. 62B

ALIASES : Giuseppe Cantalanotte; Joe Catalanoa; Joe Cantalanote; Cock-eyed Joe.

DESCRIPTION : Born in Palermo, Italy, March 8, 1900; white, male; height 5'6"; weight 162 lbs; complexion sallow; hair black; eyes brown; build medium; wears glasses and the left eye is artificial.

LOCALITIES FREQUENTED : Resides at 4434 Burns St; Original Lunch & Gay Bar, 2616 Gratiot Ave; Barasi's Grocery Store, 2701 Chene St; East Detroit Auto Wash, 23454 Gratiot Ave; Fairgrounds Race Track, all in Detroit, Michigan.

CRIMINAL ASSOCIATES : Sam Caruso; Angelo Meli; Black Tony Termine; Mike Rubino; Paul Cimino; Peter Guardino, all of Detroit, Mich; John Ormento & Joe Tocco of NYC.

FACSIMILE OF SIGNATURE

Federal Bureau of Narcotics file on Joe Catalanotte. *National Archives.*

Giannola and Vitale factions and not long after assumed the position of boss. Catalanotte was a forward-thinking gangster and believed wide-scale gangland violence was bad for business. The Italians certainly committed violent acts against rivals and deadbeats, yet within the organization, Catalanotte's philosophy greatly reduced infighting.

At the time, Detroit's mafia existed as a set of regional sections. Singing Sam's old crew was considered part of the Westside region. His brother Giuseppe "Cockeyed Joe" Catalanotte was the group leader. Cockeyed Joe was a rough customer, known as a hit man, bootlegger and convicted dope smuggler. Other members included Vincenzo "Jimmy" Catalanotte and union busters Onofrio "Nono" Minaudo and Santo Perrone.

Chester LaMare was another important Westside group leader. The vice lord of Hamtramck was a barrel-chested mobster and fierce Catalanotte loyalist. LaMare's crew included "Black" Leo Cellura and Joe Amico. Cellura had the political connections while Amico made people disappear. Angelo Meli, however, was the most important member of the crew. Meli was from San Cataldo, Sicily. He co-owned the Whip Café in Hamtramck with "Black" Leo. Meli had an extensive arrest record, including concealed weapons, armed robbery, extortion, murder, bootlegging, kidnapping and larceny charges. He was a crafty gangster, however, and incurred only one conviction.

Mugshot of Detroit mafia captain Joe Tocco. *Walter P. Reuther Library.*

Joe Tocco was the last Westside group leader. He captained a violent crew of Wyandotte bootleggers. Tocco had a lengthy arrest record of his own, including drug possession, bootlegging, tax evasion, insurance fraud and murder. Like Angelo Meli, Tocco managed to avoid conviction. His crew included mob enforcers Joe Locano and Tony D'Anna.

Joe Tocco's crew was not the only group operating in the downriver area. The infamous River Gang controlled a large amount of the illegal liquor trade along the Detroit River and was considered part of the Eastside faction. Among others, gang members included "Scarface" Joe Bommarito, Peter Licavoli and Joe "Misery" Moceri.

Vito "Black Bill" Tocco controlled rackets on the east side of Detroit. Tocco was born in Terrasini, Sicily, and immigrated to the United States in 1912. He even served a stint in the U.S. Army. As a mobster, he preferred operating in the shadows, concealing his illicit gains within layers of legitimate business investments. Black Bill owned a bakery and a produce business. He was also part owner of Lakeshore Boats and Lafayette Motors. The Eastside crew also featured trigger men like "Machinegun" Pete Corrado and Tony Ruggirello.

Black Bill's right-hand man was Joe "Uno" Zerilli. The men were brothers-in-law (Vito Tocco married Zerilli's sister). Like Tocco, Zerilli was born in Terrasini and immigrated to the United States as a young man. He got his

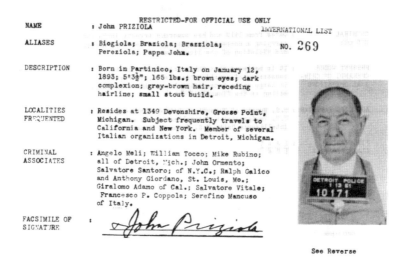

RESTRICTED-FOR OFFICIAL USE ONLY

NAME	: John PRIZIOLA
	INTERNATIONAL LIST
ALIASES	: Biogiola; Braziola; Brazziola; NO. 269
	Pereziola; Pappa John.
DESCRIPTION	: Born in Partinico, Italy on January 12, 1893; 5'3½"; 165 lbs.; brown eyes; dark complexion; grey-brown hair, receding hairline; small stout build.
LOCALITIES FREQUENTED	: Resides at 1349 Devonshire, Grosse Point, Michigan. Subject frequently travels to California and New York. Member of several Italian organizations in Detroit, Michigan.
CRIMINAL ASSOCIATES	: Angelo Meli; William Tocco; Mike Rubino; all of Detroit, Mich.; John Ormento; Salvatore Santoro; of N.Y.C.; Ralph Galico and Anthony Giordano, St. Louis, Mo.; Giralomo Adamo of Cal.; Salvatore Vitale; Francesco P. Coppola; Serefino Mancuso of Italy.
FACSIMILE OF SIGNATURE	: *John Priziola*

See Reverse

Federal Bureau of Narcotics file on "Papa" John Priziola. *National Archives.*

start in the underworld as a chauffeur and bodyguard for Sam Giannola. Zerilli was only twenty-three years old when federal investigators described him as "notorious." He started off as a driver, gunman and counterfeiter, yet by 1930, Joe Uno was the rising star of eastside gangsters.

"Papa" John Priziola was another Eastside faction leader. Priziola was born into a mafia family in Partinico, Sicily. He led a crew of fellow Partinicese gangsters. The crew was involved in bootlegging, gambling, narcotics and labor racketeering. Important members included infamous drug trafficker Frankie "Three-Fingers" Coppola, Sam Finazzo and feared mob enforcer Raffaele "Jimmy Q" Quasarano.

Remarkably, the thirty-six-year-old Sam Catalanotte kept this collection of deadly rogues in line for almost a decade. The foundations of mafia unity, however, started to crack in the winter of 1930. In early February, Singing Sam developed cold-like symptoms that turned out to be pneumonia. The mafia kingpin died from natural causes on February 14. Typical of a mafia don, Catalanotte went out in style, buried in a $10,000 casket.

Because he died unexpectedly, Singing Sam did not name a successor. To maintain stability, Detroit's mafia section leaders had to agree on a new boss. The mafia captains picked a man known as "the peacemaker." Within months, however, the consensus began to fracture, ushering in a new wave of street violence. And by breaking the peace, Motor City mobsters ended up triggering a wider mafia war in New York City.

EARLY ORGANIZED CRIME IN DETROIT

THE FISH MARKET MURDERS

Detroit gangsters referred to Gaspare Milazzo as "the peacemaker." The name was ironic considering he was a member of the old Good Killers gang. Milazzo was born in Castellammare del Golfo and a staunch ally of the Magaddino-Bonventre alliance. Milazzo was operating in the Brooklyn area, but when the Good Killers murder investigations heated up, there was too much scrutiny on the East Coast. To avoid the heat, the Castellammarese gangster relocated to the Motor City.

Once in Detroit, Milazzo linked up with Sam Catalanotte. Singing Sam was from Alcamo, Sicily. Alcamo and Castellammare were neighboring towns, and it was common for Mafiosi from the two areas to work together. Milazzo was a veteran of the Buccellato/Magaddino wars and fought in Sicily and Brooklyn. Consequently, he earned the respect of Detroit Mafiosi from the different sections. Catalanotte appointed him to a high-ranking position, though it is unclear if Milazzo was underboss or *consigliere*.

When the boss of a crime family was unavailable to govern, either because he was incarcerated or died (from natural causes or otherwise), the crime family picked an "acting boss." The acting boss assumed an intermediate position of leadership to maintain the integrity of the overall organization. When Singing Sam passed away, his brother Cockeyed Joe would have been a candidate for acting boss, but he was serving time at Leavenworth. Meanwhile, the other group leaders did not view Jimmy Catalanotte as leadership material. Gaspare Milazzo was a natural choice for the position. Held in great esteem by his mafia colleagues, "the peacemaker" also had a knack for conflict resolution.

Though he kept to himself, his neighbors realized he was an important man. They noted how the new boss drove expensive cars and wore diamond rings. The peacemaker would hold court at the Milazzo residence. At all hours of the day, it was common to see dozens of men congregating at the house, each man driving a showier car than the next. Neighbors found this interesting, especially since Milazzo had no legitimate source of income.

The fact that Milazzo maintained positive relationships with other national crime families enhanced the stature of the Detroit organization. He was close with other Castellammarase mafia bosses like Maranzano in Brooklyn and Stefano Magaddino in Buffalo. Milazzo also developed a strong alliance with Chicago Mafioso Joe Aiello. The peacemaker was godfather to Aiello's son.

Yet these relationships also meant the Detroit organization could get tangled up in national gangland conflicts. For example, Joe Aiello was

Hamtramck vice lord Chester LaMare and his wife, Anna. *Scott M. Burnstein collection.*

feuding with Chicago's mob boss "Scarface" Al Capone. To sort out these matters, Aiello invited New York godfather Joe Masseria to a meeting. The underworld referred to such meetings as "sit-downs." Aiello did not completely trust Masseria, so to balance things out, Gaspare Milazzo was invited too. During the discussions, Joe the Boss explained he would rein in Capone in exchange for some of Aiello's territory. Aiello was insulted by the offer and, for his own safety, suggested Masseria leave the Windy City.

As Aiello's men and Capone's gang continued battling, the streets were also tense in Detroit. Milazzo was the acting boss, yet Chester LaMare viewed himself as the natural heir to Catalanotte. Big Chet ran a fearsome crew, generated a lot of income for the organization and was Singing Sam's trusted mafia captain. Sporting such a résumé, LaMare believed he was the best choice for boss. One thing his fellow gangsters probably did not know, however, was that LaMare was a confidential informant for the United States Secret Service. In 1927, he was convicted of violating Prohibition laws along with Hamtramck mayor Peter Jezewski. Big Chet received a lenient sentence largely due to his status as a federal informant.

LaMare presumed other group leaders remained unaware of his duplicity, so he pushed for the top position in the organization. If the other mafia captains did not recognize his superiority, then Big Chet was going to convince them the old-fashioned way: he would just take over. LaMare started muscling in on the gambling, liquor and drug rackets of other Detroit Mafiosi. Joe Tocco from Wyandotte and the Catalanotte brothers supported Big Chet. Yet LaMare lost support within his own crew. Tired of his highhandedness, Angelo Meli and "Black" Leo Cellura defected to the Eastside faction.

In the meantime, a cold war was developing in New York between the Masseria organization and the Castellammarese mafia. And Joe the Boss was now publicly supporting Capone in Chicago and LaMare in Detroit. National alliances developed with Masseria, Capone and LaMare on one side and Maranzano, Aiello and Milazzo on the other.

Back in Detroit, Chester LaMare called for a sit-down with his old comrade Angelo Meli. LaMare's camp suggested the two sides should work things out before it turned ugly. Naturally, the peacemaker Gaspare Milazzo would oversee the meeting. Big Chet also invited Eastside gangsters Vito Tocco, Joe Zerilli and Tony Ruggirello. He suggested they meet at the Vernor Highway Fish Market owned by underworld associate Philip Guastello.

The meeting was scheduled for May 31, 1930. From LaMare's perspective, the peace summit was a sham. He viewed it as an opportunity to pull off a slaughter similar to Capone's St. Valentine's Day Massacre in Chicago. Angelo Meli and the other Eastsiders smelled a rat and pulled out at the last minute. Gaspare Milazzo, however, arrived with fellow Castellammarese Mafioso Sam Parrino. Waiting for others to arrive, Milazzo and Parrino were eating lunch near the back of the market when at least two shabbily dressed men entered and started shooting. Milazzo was shot twice in the neck and three times in the head. The forty-three-year-old mob boss died instantly. Parrino was hit in the chest and arm and transported to Receiving Hospital. Police took an antemortem statement from Parrino. Adhering to the gangster code, the victim claimed he did not recognize the shooters and did not know why anyone would shoot him or his lunch partner.

The Fish Market murders turned out to be a serious miscalculation on the part of the Westside faction. Chester LaMare may have eliminated the boss, yet Angelo Meli and his Eastside allies escaped unharmed. Furthermore, by killing Gaspar Milazzo, LaMare ignited a nationwide conflict known as the Castellammarese War.

The Killing Season

Salvatore Maranzano was outraged that someone executed his trusted *amici* (friends) in Detroit. High-ranking Castellammarese Mafiosi from Brooklyn and Buffalo held a meeting to discuss the Fish Market murders. Among those in attendance included Maranzano, Stefano Magaddino, Joe Bonanno, Vito Bonventre and Joe Parrino (Sam's brother). Maranzano viewed the shootings as a declaration of war against all Castellammaresi. The Sicilian don framed the argument to convince his men that Joe Masseria was behind the Detroit killings. There was no question that Joe the Boss supported Chester LaMare, but it was unlikely Masseria orchestrated the hit. Maranzano had his own Machiavellian motives to suggest otherwise. He coveted the top spot in the New York City underworld and knew Masseria stood in his way. The Fish Market murders presented a convenient opportunity for Maranzano to argue that war was the only option.

Masseria's organization realized war was imminent and decided to strike first. On July 15, 1930, they hit former Good Killers leader and Brooklyn mobster Vito Bonventre. He was in his garage when someone shot him in the back.

Back in the Motor City, Detroiters referred to the month as "Bloody July." It started with the July 3 killings of Cannon and Collins in front of

It was common for Detroit Police to find dozens of weapons during raids. *Walter P. Reuther Library.*

the LaSalle Hotel. On July 7, Salvatore and Giuseppe Gaglio were shot to death. The brothers were members of the LaMare crew. In retaliation, the Westside faction cut down Salvatore Cilluffo on July 12. Cilluffo was from Terrasini and aligned with the Tocco/Zerilli crew.

Other July casualties included undercover cop Barney Roth and bootlegger Johnny Mietz. The men were gunned down at Roth's Hamtramck home. Cockeyed Joe Catalanotte and Elmer Macklin were the lead suspects. Macklin was the most important non-Italian gangster to join forces with the Westside faction. Not long after the Buckley murder, police launched a raid on Catalanotte's Grosse Pointe home and arrested Cockeyed Joe and Macklin along with Joe Locano. During the raid, police found a large cache of arms and ammunition hidden in the walls. Police confiscated over fifty weapons and linked four of them to unsolved murders. Catalanotte and Macklin were tried for the Roth and Mietz murders but were acquitted.

The blow-for-blow killings continued in New York, and as a result, crime families required a steady arms supply. Angelo Meli worked out a deal to supply the Castellammaresi with machine guns. Meli was president of the Detroit-based Capitol Coal Company and used it as his headquarters. The company would order guns and ammunition from a sporting goods store in New York and arrange for Maranzano's men to pick up the shipments. Police busted up the arms ring when they arrested Joe Bonanno on October 26. Bonanno, Sebastiano "Buster" Domingo and Charlie DiBenedetto arrived at the sporting goods warehouse to pick up guns, unaware the place was under surveillance. Legendary mafia hit man "Buster" Domingo was born in Castellammare del Golfo but raised in Benton Harbor, Michigan.

Joe Amico was tried for the murder of Gaspare Milazzo. *Walter P. Reuther Library.*

Charlie DiBenedetto was Maranzano's chauffeur and had an indirect Detroit connection. His relative Antonio DiBenedetto was killed by the Buccellatos in 1917. Outside the warehouse, police nabbed Bonanno and DiBendetto; Domingo managed to escape. Investigators in Detroit raided the Capitol Coal Company offices but found nothing incriminating.

A few weeks earlier, Joe Amico and Joe Locano had been tried for the murder of Gaspare Milazzo. The prosecutor described it as "one of the most important murder trials in the history of the city." During the proceedings, police arrested one of the witnesses. Benny "the Ape" Sebastiano was also having lunch at the market that day. Investigators believed he was either a spotter or one of the actual shooters. He was charged for the double murder of Milazzo and Parrino. Defense attorney Emil Colombo (Louis Colombo's son) called for a mistrial. He argued that this was an example of witness intimidation. The judge ruled against Colombo, and the trial continued.

Initially, eyewitnesses claimed they saw Amico and Locano shoot Milazzo and Parrino. Another witness claimed he saw the men run out of the market and jump into a sedan parked out front. As the trial continued, however, witnesses became less sure of their testimonials. One witness, for example, claimed he saw only the backs of the men and was no longer sure it was Amico and Locano. The prosecution's case fell apart, and both men were acquitted.

BIG CHET'S FALL

Despite all the killings, Big Chester LaMare survived 1930. The Eastside faction plotted numerous traps, but the Hamtramck crime boss was a slippery target. After the Fish Market shootings, LaMare spent little time in Detroit, hiding out in New York and Louisville, Kentucky. His time was running out, though. While he was gone, more of his supporters abandoned the cause. Big Chet was unaware, but the Catalanotte brothers made peace with the Eastside groups. Although Joe Tocco stood by LaMare, prominent members of his crew like Tony D'Anna jumped over to the Eastside faction.

Big Chet returned to his Detroit home in early February 1931. The eight room LaMare house functioned as a compound. German shepherds guarded the parameter, and inside the house, LaMare stashed three .38 pistols, two .45-caliber handguns, one .25-caliber pistol, one shotgun, one rifle, one hand grenade and 2,500 rounds of ammunition. The crime boss was being extra cautious and trusted only a few Westside mobsters.

On February 6, Big Chet and his bodyguard Joe Girardi sat in LaMare's kitchen drinking coffee when the boss complained that he was not feeling well. He asked his wife, Anna, to visit the pharmacy and pick up medication. LaMare also asked her to drive Girardi home. According to the wife, she was not gone long and returned home only to find her husband's bullet-ridden body in the kitchen. LaMare had been assassinated.

"Go into the kitchen and look at what they've done to my husband!" screamed Anna LaMare. Investigators arrived at the murder scene and

Joe Zerilli and Vito "Black Bill" Tocco were arrested for the murder of Chester LaMare. They were both released. *Scott M. Burnstein collection.*

noticed a number of clues right away. Detectives recognized that in his last moments, LaMare had been with someone he trusted. He was unarmed and felt comfortable enough to turn his back on the person. LaMare was shot at close range, his body stretched across the kitchen floor. He suffered one shot behind the ear and one through the cheek.

Police noticed something else peculiar about the scene. The blood around LaMare's neck was already congealed when police arrived. That seemed odd considering Anna LaMare claimed she stepped out for only a brief trip to the pharmacy. When confronted, she changed her story and said she was gone for almost three hours. Anna was arrested on murder charges but eventually released.

Police launched a raid on Black Bill Tocco's Grosse Pointe home the next day. Joe Zerilli was there and also arrested. Investigators rightly concluded that Tocco and Zerilli orchestrated the hit, but proving it was another matter. Both men were released.

By October, police finally had more suspects in their cross hairs. Forensic evidence linked fingerprints found in the kitchen to Joe Amico, Joe Girardi and Elmer Macklin. Investigators believed the three Westside gunmen sold out their boss and executed him in his own home. Law enforcement arrested the men, and their trial began on April 27, 1932. Without eyewitnesses, however, the murder case was on unstable ground. Originally, a mistrial was declared, and charges against Girardi were dismissed. Charges were reinstated against Amico and Macklin, yet on June 9, 1932, the jury found the men not guilty.

MEET THE NEW BOSS

With LaMare out of the way, Detroit's mafia family reemerged as a cohesive unit. The other mafia captains voted in Black Bill Tocco as the new boss. Like his predecessor Gaspare Milazzo, Tocco was respected throughout national circles.

In New York, the Castellammarese suffered a few more casualties before the war ended. Joe Parrino (Sam's brother) was killed by his own people. Maranzano viewed him as a traitor. The Castellammaresi believed Parrino made a deal with Masseria and LaMare to sacrifice his own brother at the Fish Market shootings.

After the death of Masseria, Salvatore Maranzano declared himself boss of all bosses. Lucky Luciano was guaranteed Masseria's rackets as part of

Vito "Black Bill" Tocco was the Detroit godfather during early to mid-1930s. *Walter P. Reuther Library.*

the deal. Maranzano planned on double-crossing Luciano, but Lucky was cunning and saw it coming. The Castellammarese godfather did not like that Luciano had so many non-Sicilians in his inner circle. Luciano's ruling council included Neopolitan gangsters Vito Genovese and Joe Adonis and Calabrese mobster Frank Costello. Even more offensive to Maranzano, Luciano worked with Jewish gangsters Bugsy Siegel and Meyer Lansky.

Luciano outsmarted the old Sicilian don, and on September 10, 1931, men posing as IRS agents entered Maranzano's Manhattan office and assassinated the boss. Luciano declared there would be no more boss of bosses; instead, the heads of the crime families in New York City, Buffalo and Chicago formed a mafia ruling body known as the commission. The mafia commission eventually added a seat for the Detroit crime family.

Under Tocco's leadership, the Detroit organization took advantage of the underworld stability. The Italian mafia dominated the vice trades in the city, and now they hoped to infiltrate the legitimate economy.

CHAPTER 10

GANGSTER INDUSTRIAL COMPLEX

In 1931, John Ingraham sued the shareholders of Mueller Processes Company for $700. Mueller was a chemical company based in St. Johns, Michigan. Ingraham used to be the company's bookkeeper and sought compensation for unpaid services. Curt Mueller had already dissolved the corporation by the time Ingraham brought his suit. Defendants argued there were no assets left, so the suit was pointless. On the surface, the case seemed straightforward. When reporters dug a bit deeper, however, the Mueller Processes Company revealed an interesting group of investors.

Years earlier, the company's founder, Curt Meuller, had invented an antifreeze additive for gasoline. He hoped to mass produce the additive but first needed investors. Fortunately for Meuller, prominent Detroiters lined up to invest. Judge Edward Jeffries, for example, joined the company. Jeffries presided over the Detroit Recorder's Court. His son invested in the company, along with the Recorder's Court chief deputy clerk, Julius Deutelbaum.

Meuller required more capital, so Jeffries introduced the chemist to Tony D'Anna. D'Anna invested $20,000 and invited Black Bill Tocco and Papa John Priziola to invest as well. The fact that the judge and gangster were acquaintances seemed inappropriate at best. Meuller later testified that Jeffries and D'Anna drove to St. Johns together on many occasions, something the judge confirmed. The unusual partnership did not raise any eyebrows, so the company continued with business as usual.

To move forward, the company needed permission from the federal government to manufacture industrial-grade alcohol. Meuller recruited

Jeffries in the first place hoping the judge could finesse the application process. Jeffries met with federal officials in Washington, D.C., and explained the situation. The feds, however, raised concern about the company's unseemly investors. The Bureau of Prohibition ruled it would not grant any permits unless Mueller removed gangster elements from the corporation.

After the ruling, D'Anna, Tocco and Priziola sold their shares back to Jeffries. Curiously, the Mueller laboratories were burglarized not long after. According to news reports, "Everything was stolen." The company went under, but the Ingraham lawsuit brought the bizarre business arrangement to the public's attention.

Jeffries dismissed the notion that he did anything improper. "There is nothing in this case," he told reporters. The judge claimed the case was a political witch hunt organized by his opponents. Critics blamed Jeffries for the Buckley murder case acquittals.

The judge survived a brief public scandal, yet the case highlighted a growing trend in Detroit's underworld. Mobsters were no longer content

Tony D'Anna cultivated a close relationship with Harry Bennett. Even after Bennett retired, D'Anna's companies continued working with Ford Motor Company. *Walter P. Reuther Library.*

running vice rackets and corrupting public officials. Gangsters had infiltrated the legitimate economy, and their influence extended to the heart of Detroit's industrial economy.

THE LITTLE GUY

Harry Bennett was at the center of Detroit's criminal-industrial nexus. At five-foot-five, 150 pounds, Bennett was known as "the Little Guy." Few called Bennett that to his face, however. Connected to players in the upperworld and underworld, the Little Guy was Henry Ford's right-hand man. A former boxer and navy veteran, Bennett was the second most powerful person at Ford Motor Company. Henry Ford even backed Bennett as he jousted with Edsel Ford for control of the company. Overall, he was one of the most colorful figures in the history of industrial Detroit.

Bennett and Ford met under unusual circumstances. Ford was in New York to be interviewed by famous newspaper editor Arthur Brisbane. Ford and Brisbane were at Battery Park when a fight broke out. The police arrived to break up the mêlée, yet one brawler proved especially difficult to restrain. The automotive magnate was impressed at how Harry Bennett handled himself while scuffling with the cops. Ford told the authorities he could rehabilitate the scrappy young man. He also explained to Bennett that he needed more tough guys at Ford Motor Company. The diminutive brawler accepted Ford's offer and eventually became the tycoon's head of security.

Bennett started off as a type of manager without portfolio. He acted as Ford's bodyguard, chauffeur and all around problem solver. Soon Bennett was head of the Ford Service Department, the world's largest private security force at the time. Part of his job was gathering intelligence. Ford was violently opposed to unionization, and Bennett was in charge of keeping unions out of the Ford plants. The Service Department had spies throughout the factories. They implemented a "no-talking" rule on the assembly line because the old man feared workers would talk about collective bargaining.

Bennett spied on not only the rank and file but also management. When meeting with Ford executives, Bennett would arrange for his assistant to call him out of the office for a moment. Though his office was Spartan, he did have a portrait of his daughter on the wall. Behind the portrait was a running microphone. Getting called out of the office was a ruse designed to get his colleagues to speak unguarded while the microphone

Left to right: Henry Ford II, Harry Bennett and Henry Ford. *Walter P. Reuther Library.*

recorded everything. Bennett also conducted target practice in his office. It was common for Bennett to interrupt meetings with colleagues, pull out his .45-caliber handgun and start shooting targets. Henry Ford would join him on occasion.

When Bennett wanted to intimidate his guests, he used his personal office, but when he needed to schmooze with clients, he would take them up to his third-floor dining room. The room was the opposite of his austere private office. Here one found luxurious sofas, exotics rugs, expensive furniture and an impressive fireplace.

Bennett liked the finer things in life. Although Ford Motor Company paid him a modest salary, Henry Ford gave his right-hand man millions of dollars worth of real estate. Bennett owned a hunting lodge on Harsens Island and the famous mansion in Ann Arbor known as "the Castle." The mansion featured spiral staircases, hidden doors, escape tunnels, gun towers and a lion's den with actual lions.

The Little Guy especially liked to entertain at his mansion on Grosse Isle. An assortment of judges, politicians and local police chiefs would visit the island home and seek Bennett's favor. In many ways, he

Henry Ford's notorious right-hand man, Harry Bennett. *Walter P. Reuther Library.*

resembled the old Detroit political bosses like Ferdinand Palma and Billy Boushaw. Ford biographer Carol Gelderman explained the source of Bennett's political power: "Most state officials in Dearborn or Detroit could not run for office without a petition with a specified number of signatures. All Bennett had to do for someone he wanted to ingratiate himself with was to put a petition on the conveyor belt, and by the end of the shift the prospective candidate had all the signatures he needed." Ironically, the ex-pugilist accumulated so much political power that Henry Ford hired former police chief John Gillespie to spy on the spymaster.

Bennett bragged that racketeers were just as likely as public officials to attend his soirées. Both Ford and Bennett were fascinated by crime. The two fancied themselves amateur detectives and often meddled in local police investigations. Ford also believed in rehabilitation. By this time,

Bennett was heading up the Rouge Employment Office. Ford instructed his number two man to hire ex-convicts as part of a rehabilitation effort. The automotive tycoon's penchant for offering criminals a second chance was curious considering he was a social Darwinist. Ford opposed labor unions and social welfare programs, even at the height of the Great Depression. Regardless, he hoped that employing such men would keep them out of trouble. Bennett followed orders, and eventually 20 percent of Ford's workforce had criminal records.

Bennett channeled a lot of convicts into his security force. He hired a number of gangsters, including Sam Caruso and Legs Laman. The Ford Service Department employed such men to form an anti-union goon squad. Bennett's union busters attacked labor activists on numerous occasions. One high-profile battle took place on March 7, 1932, when five thousand protestors staged a hunger march outside the Rouge factory. Bennett's men arrived and assaulted the protestors. Predictably, local police sided with Ford Motor Company and went after the labor activists. Police opened fire and killed four protestors. The scene nearly repeated itself five years later during the "Battle of the Overpass." Activists with the United Auto Workers, including Walter Reuther, were attacked by Bennett's men while distributing pro-labor literature at the Rouge Factory.

Henry Ford wanted to employ mobsters not only to bust up unions but also to protect his own family from kidnappers. The so-called snatch racket was prevalent in Detroit during the 1920s and 1930s. In some cases, gangs would kidnap other mobsters; however, children of wealthy businessmen were more lucrative targets. Ford was especially concerned that someone would target his grandchildren. He ordered Bennett to start cultivating relationships with more underworld characters as a means to safeguard the family.

Bennett's first big gangster hire was Joseph "Legs" Laman. The Little Guy's initial encounter with the bandit was a memorable one. Laman was suspected of being involved in the kidnapping of David Cass. The victim was from an old, wealthy Detroit family. Kidnappers demanded $25,000 for David's release. The Cass family was friendly with the Fords, so Henry asked Bennett to look into the matter. Bennett began asking his underworld contacts if they knew anything, and eventually Laman found out. One evening Bennett was driving home in his Lincoln when he noticed a car heading toward him with its headlights off. He was street smart enough to recognize the situation as a potential drive-by shooting. As the car approached, Bennett ducked down, and sure enough one of the occupants in the other car pointed his double-barreled shotgun at the Lincoln. The man fired and blew out Bennett's windshield. Bennett pulled over, and none other than Legs Laman walked over to him and shoved a shotgun in his gut. "You SOB, you're looking for information, aren't you?" asked the bandit chief. Bennett talked his way out of being killed and agreed to back off. David Cass's body was later found in the Flint River.

In 1929, Legs Laman was tried and convicted of another kidnapping and received a thirty-year sentence at Jackson State Prison. While incarcerated, his gang promised to take care of his wife and children. Laman soon realized that was an empty promise. Feeling betrayed by his old comrades, the outlaw agreed to cooperate with authorities and provide information about his own gang.

As part of the plea agreement, Laman was released from prison on one condition: he had to hold a legitimate job. Harry Bennett figured he had just the right position for the kidnapper extraordinaire. He worked out a deal with the prosecutor, and Legs Laman went to work for the Ford Service Department. Bennett explained to his new employee that he felt obligated to help him considering Laman had spared his life that one evening. The bandit chief replied, "Oh, no. If I'd had another slug in my gun, you'd have got it."

MOBBED UP

Bennett worked out similar deals to help other gangsters with their legal troubles. Henry Ford was fascinated by Chester LaMare. When he found out LaMare was busted for violating Prohibition laws, Ford put his right-hand man on the case. Bennett contacted Joseph Palma, a Detroit businessman and former Secret Service agent. When Palma was a federal agent, LaMare was his prized confidential informant. Now that Big Chet was in trouble, Palma wanted to help. Palma negotiated with the court, and LaMare received probation rather than jail-time. Part of the deal was LaMare would work for Ford Motor Company.

Unsurprisingly, Big Chet did not take a position on the assembly line. Instead, LaMare received a contract to supply the Rouge factory with concession stands. This was a lucrative deal considering the Rouge employed 100,000 workers. One of LaMare's front men ran the operation. When congressional investigators asked if the mob boss actually worked at the stands, Bennett laughed and said, "LaMare didn't know a banana from an orange."

Harry Bennett testifies before the Kefauver Congressional Hearings. *Walter P. Reuther Library.*

Big Chet brought along his Westside mob partner Joe Tocco. In addition to having a monopoly on concessions, the mobsters ran a million-dollar gambling operation inside the Rouge. Congressional investigators found that inside the factory, "gambling was going on virtually everywhere." The mob ran large-scale sports betting operations and lotteries inside the plant. On the surface, the situation seemed odd, considering the Service Department kept workers under obsessive surveillance to make sure they did not unionize. Yet the same security teams looked the other way when it came to gambling. The situation made sense, however, when one realized Bennett had become rather chummy with LaMare and Tocco. According to Bennett, mob guys used to visit his office frequently. "These fellows came in like flies in and out," he recalled. Big Chet and Joe Tocco even used the word "boss" as a term of affection for Bennett.

The arrangement was disrupted when LaMare was assassinated in 1931. Wyandotte-based gangster Tony D'Anna viewed this as opportunity. For years, he had resented the way LaMare and Tocco monopolized the contracts and gambling rackets at Ford. Even though he was part of the Wyandotte crew, D'Anna sided with the Eastside faction during the Castellammarese War. With LaMare gone, Joe Tocco lost favor with the Detroit crime family's ruling class. As a result, Tony D'Anna was put in charge of the Wyandotte rackets. His first order of business was to eliminate Joe Tocco and take over the Ford action.

Wyandotte-based Mafioso Joe Tocco, circa 1931. *Walter P. Reuther Library.*

Bennett heard about this and intervened. He met with D'Anna and worked out a deal. If he spared Tocco's life, Ford Motor Company would grant D'Anna a lucrative auto transportation contract. D'Anna owned 50 percent of E&L Auto Transport. The new Wyandotte mafia captain agreed to the offer. Bennett granted E&L an exclusive contract to transport cars from the Rouge factory. The bargain reeked with impropriety considering D'Anna had a criminal record, very little capital and no prior experience in the automotive business. Bennett was unapologetic and told his critics this was part of Ford's rehabilitation agenda. Bringing gangsters into the legitimate economy kept them out of trouble, in his view.

Associating with gangsters was a public service according to Bennett's twisted logic. He did, however, negotiate the surrender of one of Michigan's

Infamous mob enforcer "Black" Leo Cellura. *Walter P. Reuther Library.*

most dangerous fugitives. Ted Pizzino and Angelo Livecchi were acquitted of the Buckley murder, but they were convicted of committing the other La Salle Hotel murders. On June 27, 1931, the court convicted Pizzino and Livechhi for the murders of William Cannon and George Collins. The state also indicted a third person in the case: Leo Cellura. Black Leo went on the lam rather than face trial. For five years, he was one of Michigan's most wanted criminals.

In July 1936, Black Leo contacted Harry Bennett and told him he wanted to surrender. Cellura wanted to avoid a hostile arrest situation and asked Bennett if he could negotiate a nonviolent surrender with the prosecutor. The Ford Service boss invited Cellura to his office to discuss the details. Bennett did not think to tell anyone he had already scheduled lunch with Michigan governor Frank Fitzgerald on the same day. The gangster and the governor arrived at the same time, and Fitzgerald sat through one of the most awkward lunches of his career. The governor was furious with Bennett and thought it was some type of blackmail scheme.

As for Black Leo, Bennett negotiated a peaceful surrender. Cellura eventually faced his day in court and claimed he shot Cannon and Collins in self-defense. The jury did not buy it, and Cellura was found guilty.

EARLY ORGANIZED CRIME IN DETROIT

Harry Bennett was wheeling and dealing with Detroit mobsters but soon realized how precarious the partnership had become. The Rouge plant had its own thirty-man fire department. In reality, it was part of Bennett's union-busting security force. The so-called fire squad was staffed with Peter Licavoli's men. Ford paid for its services, and Licavoli received a cut. After a while, the River Gang boss told John Gillespie that he wanted his men to receive a fifteen-dollar-a-day wage, which was a substantial increase. The mobster also demanded a larger finder's fee for staffing the fire squad. Gillespie passed the information to Harry Bennett, but the security chief was furious. "Get them out!" he shouted. Bennett fired the entire fire squad on the spot. The little guy underestimated his opponent.

Bennett was a formidable man in his own right, yet Peter Licavoli was a stone-cold killer. On March 27, 1937, Licavoli and a crew of his men forced Harry Bennett's car off the road. The car ended up in a ditch off Greenfield road in Dearborn. Bennett exited the vehicle brandishing his .45-caliber handgun. The assailants drove off, but Bennett got the message. He realized it was only a matter of time before the River Gang finished the job.

To avoid the worst, Bennett reached out to another powerful Mafioso. Joe Adonis was a high-ranking member of the Luciano crime organization in New York. Adonis was a premier East Coast gangster involved in bootlegging, gambling, extortion, narcotics and larceny. He also owned the transportation company Automotive Conveyance. The business had a contract to haul cars from the Ford Edgewater plant in New Jersey. Details are unclear, yet it is likely Joe Adonis brokered a sit-down between Bennett and Licavoli and squashed the feud.

Ford Motor Company was not the only mobbed-up industrial giant in Detroit. Stove Works was one of the major non-automotive industrial companies in the Motor City. John Fry was president of the company. Like Henry Ford, Fry desperately wanted to keep unions out of his factory. At one point, labor activists organized a major strike at the plant, and Fry had to bring in eighty police officers to guard the property. Stove Works followed Ford's template and hired its own goon squad. Whereas Ford had Harry Bennett, Fry brought in Santo Perrone. The Mafioso recruited a gang of union busters, cracked some heads and put an end to labor strife at the plant. In return, Stove Works granted Perrone a very profitable scrap-hauling contract.

SETTLING ACCOUNTS

By the late 1930s, Detroit's mafia organization was united and raking in millions of dollars in illicit profits. Prohibition was over, yet the mafia continued its profitable ventures in gambling, loan-sharking, labor racketeering, extortion, prostitution and narcotics. It even penetrated sectors of the legitimate economy.

The organization hit one snag, however, when Black Bill Tocco was convicted of tax evasion in 1936. While in prison, Tocco's right-hand man and brother-in-law, Joe Zerilli, took over as acting boss. These were prosperous years for the crime family, yet the Italian mafia had two more scores to settle.

Detroit's Italian mob was growing stronger, while the notorious Purple Gang was on a downward trajectory. A combination of infighting and incarceration weakened the Jewish syndicate. The Purple Gang did not adhere to a strict hierarchy like the mafia. Nevertheless, Abe Burnstein was the de facto Jewish mob boss of Detroit. Burnstein recognized his organization

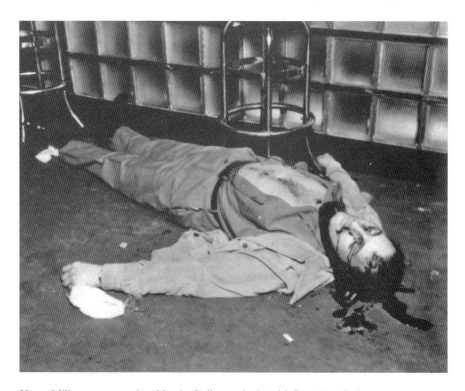

Harry Millman was murdered by the Italian mob. *Scott M. Burnstein collection.*

was on the decline and met with the Italians to discuss the underworld's new order. The Jewish gangster always had a profitable working relationship with the Italians, so the negotiations were amicable. Burnstein dissolved the Purple Gang as an autonomous syndicate and agreed that Jewish gangsters in Detroit would work for the Italians. The Purple gangster also accepted the role of unofficial adviser to Joe Zerilli.

The annexation of the Jewish mob would have been a peaceful process if not for Harry Millman. Millman was one of the Purple Gang's young Turks. He was also a prolific drinker and one of the gang's most fearsome enforcers. Millman refused to accept Burnstein's new arrangement and resented the idea that he should take orders from anyone, let alone an Italian mobster. Instead, Millman and his crew of junior Purples challenged the Italians. Out on the nightclub scene, it was common to see Millman starting fights with Detroit Mafiosi. Even more reckless, the young Turks would stick up mafia-controlled gambling dens and brothels. Burnstein warned the impulsive Millman to knock it off and work with the Italians, but his protégé would

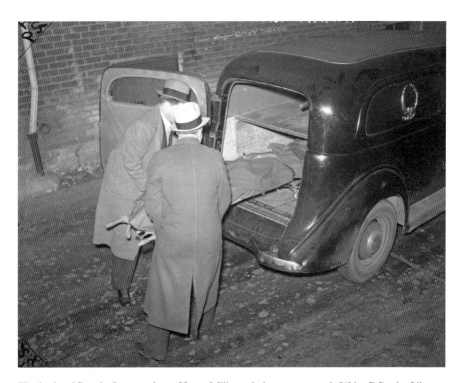

The body of Purple Gang mobster Harry Millman being transported. *Walter P. Reuther Library.*

not listen. The mafia tried to kill Millman, but he was a difficult target. Peter Licavoli and Scarface Joe Bommarito set a number of car bomb traps for Millman, yet each time the junior Purple gangster escaped harm. Surviving a series of assassination attempts only emboldened the Jewish mob enforcer.

Fate finally caught up with Millman on November 27, 1937. He was at Boesky's Restaurant in Detroit when two hit men walked in and started shooting. Millman was hit ten times. One of his men was also killed during the shooting.

Joe Tocco's time was also running out. Harry Bennett may have convinced Tony D'Anna to call off the Tocco hit in 1932, but Mafiosi are known for their patience. After LaMare's death, the crime family demoted Tocco, but he was still active in the rackets. He operated under the protection of cousin Vito Tocco. So when Black Bill went to prison for tax evasion, the downriver gangster's days were numbered.

On the early morning of May 3, 1938, at least two gunmen confronted Joe Tocco in front of his Wyandotte home. Tocco was hit with seven shotgun blasts but survived long enough to make it to Wyandotte General Hospital. As he was dying, the beer baron asked for Harry Bennett. The Ford man arrived, and Tocco asked if he was going to die. Bennett explained that he was hit badly, and it did not look good. Bennett arranged for a priest to visit the room and read Tocco his last rites.

Legacy

Removing Millman and Tocco paved the way for Detroit's crime organization to enter the 1940s with a clean slate. After Black Bill Tocco finished his prison sentence, he moved to Florida and lived in semi-retirement. Back in Detroit, Joe Zerilli was anointed the official boss of the family.

The new godfather encouraged his lieutenants to marry off their children to sons and daughters of other Mafiosi. Zerilli bargained that members of the crime family were less likely to rat on one another if they were related. His intermarriage policy also reduced the likelihood of infighting in the organization. Zerilli's strategy paid off, and Detroit's mafia family was a pillar of stability, dominating organized crime in Detroit during the 1940s and '50s.

By the 1960s and 1970s, second-generation Mafiosi with familiar names like Bommarito, Corrado, Meli, Tocco and Zerilli continued the family

Legendary Detroit godfather Joe Zerilli. He led the organization from the mid-1930s to his death in 1977. *Walter P. Reuther Library.*

business. New mobsters like the infamous Giacalone (Tony and Vito) brothers emerged as underworld heavyweights, and Detroit's mafia organization extended its influence to Las Vegas, San Diego and Tucson. Internationally, the organization played a pivotal role in facilitating the global heroin trade. Law enforcement also suspected the Detroit mob was responsible for the disappearance of famous labor leader Jimmy Hoffa. As recently as 2006, several Detroit mobsters were arrested for running a large-scale gambling operation.

Today, Detroit's crime family is not as high profile as it once was, yet the mafia tradition that began over one hundred years ago perseveres.

BIBLIOGRAPHY

Bennett, Harry, and Paul Marcus. *We Never Called Him Henry*. New York: Gold Medal Books, 1951.

Bonanno, Bill. *Bound by Honor: A Mafioso's Story*. New York: St. Martin, 2000.

Bonanno, Joseph. *A Man of Honor*. New York: Simon & Schuster, 1983.

Bryan, Ford. *Henry's Lieutenants*. Detroit, MI: Wayne State University Press, 1993.

Buccellato, James, and Scott M. Burnstein. "The Detroit Drug Pipeline." *The Detroit True Crime Chronicles*. Edited by Scott M. Burnstein. Philadelphia: Camino Books Inc., 2013.

———. "Organized Crime in Detroit: Forgotten, but Not Gone." *CBS Detroit*. (2011). http://detroit.cbslocal.com/2011/06/24/organized-crime-in-detroit-forgotten-but-not-gone.

Burnstein, Scott M. *Motor City Mafia: A Century of Organized Crime in Detroit*. Charleston, SC: Arcadia Publishing, 2006.

Conot, Robert. *American Odyssey*. Detroit, MI: Wayne State University Press, 1986.

Costanza, Salvatore. *La Patria Armata*. http://www.trapaninostra.it/libri/salvatore_costanza/La_patria_armata/S_Costanza_-_La_patria_armata_-_004.htm.

———. "La Rivolta Contra i 'Cutrara' a Castellammare del Golfo: 1862." *NQ/M* 4, no. 16 (1966): 419–38.

Critchley, David. "Buster, Maranzano and the Castellammare War: 1930–1931." *Global Crime* 7, no. 1 (2006): 43–78.

BIBLIOGRAPHY

————. *The Origin of Organized Crime in America: The New York Mafia, 1891–1931*. New York: Routledge, 2009.

Detroit Police Department. *Story of the Detroit Police Department: 1916–1917*. Detroit, MI: Detroit Police Department, 1917.

Dickie, John. *Cosa Nostra: A History of the Sicilian Mafia*. New York: Palgrave Macmillian, 2004.

Fine, Sidney. *Frank Murphy: The Detroit Years*. Ann Arbor: University of Michigan Press, 1975.

Gelderman, Carol. *Henry Ford: The Wayward Capitalist*. New York: Dial Press, 1981.

Gouth, George. *Booze, Boats & Bad Times: Recalling Wyandotte's Dark Days of Prohibition*. Wyandotte, MI: Wyandotte Historical Society, 2004.

Helmer, William J., and Rick Mattix. *The Complete Public Enemy Almanac*. Nashville, TN: Cumberland House, 2007.

Hunt, Thomas, and Mike Tona. "The Good Killers: 1921's Glimpse of the Mafia." http://www.onewal.com/a014/f_goodkillers.html.

Kavieff, Paul. *Detroit's Infamous Purple Gang*. Charleston, SC: Arcadia Publishing, 2008.

————. *The Purple Gang: Organized Crime in Detroit*. Fort Lee, NJ: Barricade Books, 2000.

————. *The Violent Years: Prohibition and the Detroit Mobs*. Fort Lee, NJ: Barricade Books, 2001.

Kowalkski, Greg. *Wicked Hamtramck: Lust, Liquor, and Lead*. Charleston, SC: The History Press, 2010.

Liggett, Walter. "Michigan: Soused and Serene." *Plain Talk* 6, no. 3, (1930): 257–74.

Lovett, William. *Detroit Rules Itself*. Boston: Gotham Press, 1930.

Martelle, Scott. *Detroit: A Biography*. Chicago: Chicago Review Press, 2012.

Mason, Philip P. *Rumrunning and the Roaring Twenties: Prohibition on the Michigan-Ontario Waterway*. Detroit, MI: Wayne State University Press. 1995.

Maxwell, Gavin. *The Ten Pains of Death*. New York: E.P. Dutton & Co., 1960.

Newark, Tim. *Boardwalk Gangster: The Real Lucky Luciano*. New York: St. Martin's Press, 2010.

Nelli, Humbert. "The Italian Padrone System in the United States." *Labor History* 5, no. 2 (1964): 153–67.

Player, Cyril Arthur. "Gangsters and Politicians in Detroit: The Buckley Murders." *Detroit Perspectives*. Edited by Wilma Henrickson. Detroit, MI: Wayne State University Press, 1991.

Reppetto, Thomas. *American Mafia*. New York: Henry Holt and Company, 2004.

BIBLIOGRAPHY

Servadio, Gaia. *Mafioso: A History of the Mafia from Its Origins to the Present Day*. New York: Stein and Day, 1976.

Talese, Guy. *Honor Thy Father*. Greenwich, CT: Fawcett Publications, 1971.

United States Treasury Department, Bureau of Narcotics. *Mafia: The Government's Secret File on Organized Crime*. New York: HarperCollins, 2007.

Vismara, John. "Coming of the Italians to Detroit." *Michigan History* 2, no. 1 (1918).

Waugh, Daniel. *Off Color: The Violent History of Detroit's Notorious Purple Gang*. Holland, MI: In-Depth Editions, 2014.

Zunz, Olivier. *The Changing Face of Inequality: Urbanization, Industrial Development, and Immigrants in Detroit, 1880–1920*. Chicago: University of Chicago Press, 1982.

GOVERNMENT DOCUMENTS

FBI Files: Antonio Magaddino

Michigan State Police. *Hamtramck, Michigan: The Present Situation*. Detroit, MI: April 28, 1924.

Recorder's Court of the City of Detroit. *The People of the State of Michigan vs. Vito Adamo and Felice Buccellato for murder* (1913).

———. *The People of the State of Michigan vs. Giovanni Torres for murder* (1918).

———. *The People of the State of Michigan vs. Joseph Buccellato for violating prohibition laws* (1919).

———. *The People of the State of Michigan vs. Calogero Arena for murder* (1920).

———. *The People of the State of Michigan vs. Joe Locano and Joe Amico for murder* (1930).

———. *The People of the State of Michigan vs. Joe Locano and Elmer Macklin for murder* (1932).

State of New York: Division of Alcoholic Beverage Council, Report of Investigation: B 8969 [Subject Stefano Magaddino], January 3, 1958.

United States Congress, Senate. Special Committee to Investigate Organized Crime in Interstate Commerce. *Investigation of Organized Crime in Interstate Commerce: Part 9 Michigan*. 81st Cong., 1st sess. Washington, D.C.: GPO, 1951.

———. Permanent Subcommittee on Investigations of the Committee on Government Operations. *Organized Crime and Illicit Traffic in Narcotics: Part 2*. 88th Cong., 1st sess. Washington, D.C.: GPO, 1963.

United States Secret Service. *Daily Reports of Agent Joseph A. Palma*, 1922.

BIBLIOGRAPHY

Newspapers

Brooklyn Daily Eagle
Detroit Free Press
Detroit News
Detroit Times
Literary Digest
New York Times

Websites

http://gangsterreport.com
http://seekingmichigan.org

INDEX

INDEX

INDEX

INDEX